BUT YOU LOOK SO WELL

The Struggle to Survive When Pain is Invisible

'No-one knows the growth she made in order to survive; she is both fierce and fragile in equal measure.'
V.J. Markham

Denise Trewartha

First published by Ultimate World Publishing 2025
Copyright © 2025 Denise Trewartha

ISBN

Paperback: 978-1-923425-55-2
Ebook: 978-1-923425-56-9

Denise Trewartha has asserted her rights under the Copyright, Designs and Patents Act 1988 to be identified as the author of this work. The information in this book is based on the author's experiences and opinions. The publisher specifically disclaims responsibility for any adverse consequences which may result from use of the information contained herein. Permission to use information has been sought by the author. Any breaches will be rectified in further editions of the book.

All rights reserved. No part of this publication may be reproduced, stored in or introduced into a retrieval system, or transmitted in any form, or by any means (electronic, mechanical, photocopying, recording or otherwise) without the prior written permission of the author. Any person who does any unauthorised act in relation to this publication may be liable to criminal prosecution and civil claims for damages. Enquiries should be made through the publisher.

Cover design: Ultimate World Publishing
Layout and typesetting: Ultimate World Publishing
Editor: Marinda Wilkinson
Photographers: Robert Dettman, David Pav, Michael Wedd and Livia Gu
Illustrations:
Usman Naeem
Adike-Shutterstock.com (Iceberg)
Alila Medical Media-Shutterstock.com (The Trigeminal Nerve)
Alila Medical Media-Shutterstock.com (The Facial Nerve)
Chu KyungMin-Shutterstock.com (Glossopharyngeal Nerve)
Chu KyungMin-Shutterstock.com (Vestibulocochlear Nerve)
In Art-Shutterstock.com (Cover)
Pikovit-Shutterstock.com (Distribution of cranial nerves)

Ultimate World Publishing
Diamond Creek,
Victoria Australia 3089
www.writeabook.com.au

TESTIMONIALS

'It's not about knowing what to say. It's about being there when nobody knows what to say. The only thing people need to hear is, "You are not alone." And that doesn't require words. It just requires your presence.'
James Clear

But You Look So Well is a gut-wrenching memoir of extreme suffering and despair, and ultimately, of resilience, emotional growth and hope. In reading it, you will cry (a lot), you will laugh (a little), but most importantly, gain some insight into the silent suffering of those with severe chronic pain or indeed any chronic illness where an outward appearance of health belies their truth. As her general medical practitioner, I have had the privilege of walking alongside Denise through her journey. She handles it with grace and humility. I admire her courage and perseverance to find a simpler life of acceptance and new meaning. I highly recommend her story to anyone with chronic pain and the people who love and care for them.

H. S., MBBS FRACGP

When people say someone wears their heart on their sleeve, what they really mean is that someone displays a vast array of emotions on their face. Facial nerve damage is a breaking of a communication and emotion conduit, made all the more stark because the damaged half of the face lives side-by-side the undamaged half.

Human beings are social creatures and this extends well beyond aesthetics and vanity. Human connection and communication are essential functions of everyday life. A simple facial expression can express a thousand words, and without it, the anxieties and insecurities of face-to-face contact become overwhelming. Reluctance to smile, hesitancy to face the person you are talking to, avoiding gatherings, social outings and work colleagues – all of these things cause a tortured introspection. Deeper than this, however, is to have lost a sense of self, of identity, of expression. It is a particularly cruel chokehold which makes facial nerve injury one of the most complex health issues to navigate. I have had the pleasure of helping Denise regain – and maintain – enough facial function to restore her confidence to laugh, smile and begin reconnecting with her sense of self.

Victoria, Neurophysiotherapist

My wife has always been deeply passionate about her career and empathetic to all people she meets. She is an incredible person, with a profound love for nature and the beauty that surrounds us. She is a soft and gentle soul, yet the horrendous nerve damage that followed her shingles outbreak revealed a resilience that continues to amaze me. Despite the ongoing pain she endures, her strength and determination to improve her quality of life has never wavered. I admire her unrelenting pursuit of every possible option to ease her suffering and find a way forward.

Witnessing the effects of chronic nerve pain on my wife has been heartbreaking. Something as simple as a light breeze on a calm day, or a drop in temperature, could send excruciating stabbing jolts through her face. I'd have understood completely if she succumbed to the effects of her condition. Yet, instead of surrendering, she fought, pushing through each day when giving up would have been the easier path. I love her not only for her

TESTIMONIALS

strength and courage but for everything she is and all she does for our family. Denise refused to give up. She sought guidance from her incredible medical professionals, looking outside the square, leaving no stone unturned in her search for relief, just to get through another day. I hope her story gives hope to others navigating similar pain journeys, and for those who haven't experienced it, a deeper understanding that pain isn't always visible, but its impact can be horrific.

John

This is indeed a special memoir, birthed out of debilitating pain and written while battling this ongoing suffering alongside a myriad of physical, psychological and emotional challenges. Beautifully crafted, one cannot read this and remain unaffected. Denise's story displays tenacious determination and courage and is recounted with a detailed honesty and raw vulnerability that makes for an intense emotional read. Her portrayal of the battle to live with her medical challenges and her quest for answers is at times harrowing and confronting, but necessary and worthwhile. It is a thought-provoking journey into 'things' unexplored and often not understood.

Reading this book is a profound and powerful experience; it teaches, enlightens and motivates. It is a book you didn't know you needed to read. It teaches you things you didn't think you needed to know. It helps you to understand things you didn't think you needed to understand. Reading this book is a valued, life-changing gift from the heart of the author, full of treasured insights. Thank you Denise. May we all seek to understand and love ourselves and others better.

Jenny

If you, as I have been, are fortunate enough to have a friend like Denise, a friend who radiates love from their very being, then hold onto them with both hands. I will be eternally grateful that our passion for education brought us together and I was able to see her lead in action. I am blessed every day to call her my friend – to see her stand today as an author is the greatest blessing of all. To see her survive. I watched, rendered speechless, as this gentle and compassionate human was viciously and swiftly attacked by shingles. Denise endured blow after blow after blow. Sidelined with nothing but love to offer, I helplessly feared for her life as her pleas for some reprieve, some comfort, were continually met with futility.

Knowing Denise has unequivocally changed how I live and approach my life and time on earth. Her honesty lifted a veil of disillusion around invisible conditions. Because of her, I strive to look at another, and really see. Ask about another, and really hear. Live consciously with self-compassion. Value life and really, truly prioritise health, both physical and emotional. To those who suffer, her story says, 'You can survive.' To those who heal, her story says, 'You are enough.' To those who merely exist in this world, her story says, 'You can create a life worth living.' Her story is a gift to the world. Please take it, hold it, pass it on.

Lisa

But You Look So Well is a deeply moving, engaging and thought-provoking memoir – at times heartbreaking, at times full of positivity and hope. Written with honesty, this profoundly personal story is a window into the soul of someone who has suffered incredibly due to an invisible chronic illness. It is a story about day-to-day survival, resilience, inner strength, courage, steely determination and self-empowerment. A journey of endurance, not a sprint. It reflects an investigative and action-based approach to chronic illness and trauma, which is the same approach my dear friend Denise has to life in general.

This memoir is a must-read for anyone who wants to understand how a friend, family member, colleague or even someone they don't actually know, suffers quietly, silently, because of an invisible illness or the impact of trauma. It provides profound insight into finding the will to live despite this and offers a glimpse of what others can do to support and sustain a similar life journey for someone, simply by showing empathy and demonstrating compassion.

Raelene

Reading about Denise's struggles has been both confronting and deeply moving. The extent of her cruel suffering is difficult to comprehend, yet she remains steadfast in her commitment to kindness and generosity. Despite enduring excruciating, electric shock-like facial pain – a hallmark of PHTN – she has chosen not to be defined by her condition. Instead of succumbing to self-pity, she sought to understand this challenge that had taken over her life, becoming not only a warrior for herself, but also sharing her knowledge and offering support to those in need.

What truly stands out is Denise's willingness to share her pain, to open up about her journey, and to make the courageous effort to regain her life. Despite her specialists acknowledging most struggle to find a way to live with it, she continues to lead with grace, strength and an unwavering spirit, facing each day with inspiring determination. Her deep care for others shines through as she shares her story, offering both compassion and insight, and proving that even in the face of adversity, there is a path to recovery and growth. As a close friend, I am in awe of her resilience. Her ability to continue moving forward, despite unimaginable hardship, fills me with profound admiration. We can all learn from her strength, generosity and unwavering commitment to others.

Kris

Watching my brave friend Denise suffer in pain, fear and isolation, conjured up a constant feeling of helplessness in me. Throughout her journey, I learnt that the best thing to do for her was to learn the art of active listening. To validate my friend, to lean in, be curious, paraphrase her information and always follow-up conversations. To do more research, reading and podcast listening to find out more about her condition. Over time, I learnt that Denise was not looking for advice or answers, she simply needed to feel heard.

Hayley

Denise's memoir, *But You Look So Well*, is a profoundly moving account of resilience in the face of pain and loss. As a close friend, reading her story was both enlightening and deeply confronting, revealing complexities I had never fully grasped. Denise has a remarkable ability to mask her struggles, often prioritising the protection and comfort of those dear to her. Yet, in writing this book, she courageously peels back the layers, sharing the raw realities and inner conflicts of living with pain.

Her journey is not just one of endurance, but of purpose, self-preservation and learning to embrace life in the moment. The wisdom woven throughout – acknowledging fears, focusing on the present and valuing health – offers powerful takeaways for anyone navigating challenges. Denise's decision to undertake such a deeply personal project is nothing short of admirable, and her determination to complete it speaks volumes about the strength that defines her. *But You Look So Well* is a testament to finding light amid adversity. It is an unforgettable read that leaves a lasting impact – one of courage, honesty and inspiration.

Sarah

I have the utmost respect and empathy for my dear friend Denise and the deeply personal journey she so bravely shares in this book. Though, I could never fully see or understand the depths of her pain, I always felt it through her stories and in the quiet strength she showed during the time we spent together. Despite the physical distance between us, I remained as close as I could. I offered my love, listening without judgement, and being a constant presence

TESTIMONIALS

whenever she needed someone to lean on. I did what I could from afar, always wishing I could do more.

Over time I witnessed a profound transformation. I saw how illness and personal trauma began to reshape her world, and how, piece by piece, she began to rebuild. What Denise has done through this journey is nothing short of remarkable. Her path to healing has been paved with resilience, courage and an unwavering determination to reclaim her life. The road she walked with countless challenges was long and often uncertain, but she faced it all with open-hearted bravery, learning and adapting to a new way of living that honoured her pain while refusing to be defined by it. Denise's courage in sharing her truth is a gift to anyone who reads it. I'm so proud of her, and moved by all that she has become.

Amanda

DEDICATION

To those living with an invisible condition – may my words offer a comforting voice of understanding for the battles you endure and for all you have lost. May the hearts and minds of your loved ones be filled with love and compassion.

To my husband and daughters – you are my light, my strength and the reason I keep going.

DISCLAIMER

This book is based on my own personal experiences and reflections. I relied on journals, recordings, medical records, letters, notes from appointments, interviews and conversations with others, as well as my own memory. In some cases, I have edited conversations for brevity. While every effort has been made to present these events accurately and authentically, names, places and identifying details have been omitted or changed to protect the privacy of individuals.

In telling my story, I am aware that I write only my story and do not presume to tell the stories of others who feature in my book. Readers should be aware that individual experiences and interpretations may vary.

The medical content is shared for informational purposes only and is not intended to diagnose, treat, cure or prevent any medical condition, and is not intended as a substitute for professional advice. Readers are encouraged to seek the guidance of qualified professionals, such as licensed therapists, counsellors or medical practitioners, if they feel the need for support.

Please note that some topics discussed in this book may be sensitive or triggering, particularly for those with lived experiences of trauma.

The author and publisher disclaim any liability for actions taken based on the information or insights shared in this book.

CONTENTS

TESTIMONIALS	iii
DEDICATION	xi
DISCLAIMER	xiii
FOREWORD: PAIN	1
FOREWORD: TRAUMA	3
DEAR READER	5
1. YOU LOOK SO WELL	9
2. THE BURNOUT	17
3. THE DIAGNOSIS	23
4. DENIAL	27
5. FEAR, SHAME AND REJECTION	35
6. GRIEF AND LOSS	43
7. REALITY SLAP	47
8. RESPONSIBILITY	53
9. DETERMINATION	63
10. ALONENESS	69
11. THE SEARCH FOR UNDERSTANDING	75
12. ACCEPTANCE	79

13.	PACING AND DISTRACTIONS	83
14.	PAIN AND IDENTITY	87
15.	ROCK BOTTOM	93
16.	BLIND HOPE	101
17.	NO STONE LEFT UNTURNED	109
18.	ALL HOPE IS GONE	115
19.	THE BOTTOM OF THE BARREL	121
20.	A LIFELINE	127
21.	LIFE SCHOOL	133
22.	THE BODY KEEPS SCORE	145
23.	TIME OUT	151
24.	MORE LOSS	161
25.	REGRESSION	165
26.	HEIDI RETURNS	169
27.	ILLUMINATE	173
28.	LIFE COACHING	187
29.	RELIEF	193
30.	REHABILITATION	203
31.	THE GAP	213
32.	A LIFE WORTH LIVING	219
	AFTERWORD	225
	ACKNOWLEDGEMENTS	227
	ABOUT THE AUTHOR	231
	TESTIMONIAL	233
	GLOSSARY	235
	BIBLIOGRAPHY	237
	ENDNOTES	239

FOREWORD: PAIN

Life is a journey, varying from tragically short to very long. Always along the way there are challenges, both positive and negative, either to the individual or to those who love them.

My professional journey in pain management has been long, with many positives and some hard-learnt negatives. This started when I was an undergraduate student with my professor of surgery, who liked to talk about the physical, psychological and social challenges of chronic pain. I'm sure many of my fellow students thought he was a crackpot and much preferred to know if there was a procedure they could do to 'cure' the problem. I found it a profound challenge and wanted to know more.

When I later joined the staff of the University of Adelaide, I was fortunate to be made an early member of the then new Chronic Pain Clinic of the Royal Adelaide Hospital. Every Wednesday afternoon we would try to diagnose and help a wide range of patients with intractable pains.

The key was to approach the issue in a multidisciplinary way by application of various combinations of medications, physical therapies and psychological counselling. With many, this approach helped. Some types of pain were more straightforward than others but the postherpetic neuralgias were always a major challenge as the viruses lived deep in the nerves and brain. The inaugural chair of the clinic was very philosophical and often stated that, 'Your pain becomes your companion in life.

If you consider it your enemy then it may destroy you, whereas if it became your constant friend, then you could go forward together.'

The professor of psychiatry was a key member of the clinic and a keen investigator of abnormal illness behaviour and life events. In brief, this meant various challenges you had experienced in life's journey could influence your pain onset and experience. I did much research along those lines and many times found this approach was a key to understanding the chronic pain journey.

These were the positive experiences in my pain journey.

The negatives are common and recurrent. Many doctors and nurses don't understand chronic pain and try to treat it like acute pain. These are two very different entities. This can lead to false hope, unnecessary procedures or blaming the patient for their misfortune. The worst are the charlatans who prey on them for pecuniary gain.

Denise, in her eloquently written book, describes her pain journey from initial hope to despair and finally deep insight. Her pain was her constant companion and became not her enemy but her friend. I commend this book to all who try to help those in need and those who suffer. Life's journey can be turned around.

Alastair Goss
Emeritus Professor of Oral & Maxillofacial Surgery

FOREWORD: TRAUMA

But You Look So Well weaves a compelling, deeply personal memoir chronicling Denise's relentless battle with facial pain brought on by shingles. It invites readers into an unflinchingly honest exploration of the subtle unfolding of such a collapse in heart-wrenching detail. Her sincere and intense journey is permeated by deep pain, both emotional and physical. She tirelessly fights this tragic life-changing attack on her nervous system with unwavering courage and determination, looking for all avenues to find relief from the debilitating pain. Her journey deeply sensitises the reader to choice points to seek various avenues of medical interventions and alternative therapies, and to engage support from friends, life coaches, therapists and support groups. Most impressively, to keep fighting for healing, normalcy and a sense of belonging in a life lived in relentless pain.

As Denise's EMDR (eye movement desensitisation and reprocessing) therapist, I had the privilege of gently assisting her to unveil and reprocess unacknowledged keystone life events. Denise bravely sat through body memories and intense emotions buried in her unconscious, gently making space for her narrative about herself, her world and some of her adaptive behaviours, which were not always helpful or true. Denise was able to develop compassion for herself, make peace with some of these events, rescript her narrative with more positive beliefs and release the charge in her nervous system.

But You Look So Well offers hope and understanding to those affected by facial pain and their loved ones. It encourages empathy and compassion through an authentic portrayal of finding help, developing personal resilience and finally embracing acceptance, all while finding moments of joy and purpose in a life irrevocably altered. It is a memoir of hope and courage, providing supportive insights for anyone navigating a similar path.

Astrid Robinson
Trauma Therapist

DEAR READER

This book you hold in your hands is more than a memoir; it's a piece of my heart. It's a story I never expected to tell, born from pain, resilience and the unyielding hope that even in our darkest moments, light can be found. Writing it has been one of the most vulnerable experiences of my life, and my hope is that it resonates with you in some way.

In 2016, my life took an unexpected turn when I contracted shingles in my face, leaving me with a debilitating condition called postherpetic trigeminal neuralgia (PHTN) and subsequently Ramsay Hunt syndrome. It's a condition marked by invisibility, relentless pain and a host of challenges that ripple through every aspect of life. But my story isn't just about illness. It's about what lies beneath the surface: the hidden struggles, the unspoken truths and the deep emotional wounds that shaped my life.

The desire to write my story came after discovering the effects of PHTN and Ramsay Hunt syndrome on others all over the world who suffer silently. Many are so crippled by the condition and live diminished lives in pain so horrific that they wish to end their lives – and some do. Initially, I set out to write a self-help book, something practical to guide others in how to live with it. A memoir was never on my radar. However, I realised how much would remain unspoken in such a format. I feared it would minimise the lived experience of those navigating this condition, reducing it to steps and strategies when, in truth, there is no single way. There are no simple answers.

I came to understand that I couldn't fully capture the reality of anyone living with this pain without sharing my story. Though I wrestled with the vulnerability and emotional weight of writing a memoir, it was the only way to honour the ongoing struggle to find a path to survival. Along the way, I also recognised how much our unique approaches to coping are shaped by past life experiences. This is *my* story. While it's a story of resilience and hope, it's also a story of the courage it takes to face life's hardest truths.

Through these pages, I share not only the physical and emotional toll of living with chronic pain but also the unexpected healing journey I undertook along the way. I delve into the impact of unresolved trauma, the ways in which we lose ourselves in the service of others, and the profound lessons that come with learning to prioritise self-love and authenticity. You'll read about my journey to reconnect with my inner child, confront old patterns of behaviour and shift long-held limiting beliefs. You'll see moments of despair and flashes of triumph, because healing – both physical and emotional – is never linear.

I wrote this book for anyone who has ever felt unseen in their pain, for those carrying the weight of invisible struggles and for anyone seeking a reminder they are not alone. My hope is that as you turn these pages, you find more than just a story – you also find a connection. A sense that someone truly understands.

In a world where invisible illnesses are often misunderstood, my story hopes to serve as a bridge to empathy and awareness, to inspire compassionate conversations with loved ones who may be silently suffering. Unfortunately, despite initiatives to increase awareness of mental health in recent years, messages like 'move on' or 'get over it' still persist, whether spoken outright or implied. Yet, simple acts of kindness, validation and a willingness to understand can create a foundation of compassion that has the power to save lives.

Writing so vulnerably about my healing journey was terrifying. However, if I wanted to raise awareness of what lies beneath the surface and honour the silent internal struggles many battle, I needed to make the invisible visible.

DEAR READER

Thank you for choosing to spend your time with my words. It's a privilege I don't take lightly and I'm grateful you've joined me on this journey. May it bring insight, comfort or simply a reminder that even in the face of what seems impossible, there is always a path forward.

BARE BONES

Hope is not always soft and lovely. She is not always cascading rivers and sunlit skies, dancing. Hope knows there is work to be done. There are roads to be travelled. Turns to be made. She is bare bones and deep waters. She is weary and weak. She is barely a glimmer. She shakes when she speaks. This is where hope lives. Smothered in sweat. Full of war. And on the verge of crumbling into the sea. Yet there she is, quietly breathing.

Ullie-Kaye
(Published with permission from the author)

1.

YOU LOOK SO WELL

*'You never know how strong you are
until being strong is your only choice.'*
Bob Marley

My face contorted in pain as the endodontist slowly moved around to face me. Despite more than two hours having passed, the myriad injections to numb my tooth and gum had been futile. I sensed his distress by the beads of sweat on his forehead. Concern and compassion emanated from this kind soul as he stopped and sympathised, 'I'm not going to continue with this procedure tonight.' Wide-eyed with terror, tears pooled in my eyes at the thought of being left in this state forever. My heart beat like a drum with the overwhelming fear I would never survive this wretched pain if it didn't stop.

This week, my tolerance had reached its peak. For days, a frightening increase in pain had been invading my mouth like someone holding a hot branding iron to it, leaving me unable to close my mouth or touch my teeth together. Every breath, the slightest movement, reminded me of something sinister, something not right, at its core. The savageness of the searing sensation had escalated throughout the week, ripping through my mouth and up into the back of my eye like a lightning bolt, rendering me barely able to speak and unable to eat.

For almost three years, neuropathic face pain, a fierce pain that could only be likened to a hot spear repeatedly pushed through my eye and ear, again and again, had been my constant companion, rising to a crescendo even in the quietest moments. There was no escape, no way of ending it. Every day, my stomach lurched at the nauseating fear it would surely take my life. A life, while diminished, I fought valiantly for. But as 2019 unfurled its wings, this punishing pain took an unexpected turn, screaming louder than ever. Amid the agony, I spent a week contemplating the origin of this persistent torment. Was it the familiar neuralgia making its erratic dance moves across my nerves? Or could it be a dental issue making its own noise within the recesses of my jaw? Whispering hopeful thoughts this could be solved, I had finally settled on the latter, prompting an urgent visit to the endodontist.

Facing me, the endodontist gently said, 'I'm concerned about proceeding with root canal treatment on you with your condition. I need to be extremely cautious and certain about the procedure required.' Knowing what I knew about trigeminal neuralgia, I understood his reservations. 'Early tomorrow morning, I want you to see an oral and maxillofacial surgeon who many of us in the dental profession consult for advice.' There was still hope. I wasn't being told there was nothing he could do.

The following morning after examining my face, the surgeon remarked, 'Well, you've certainly got the whole trifecta here.' He explained that the shingles virus, herpes zoster, had damaged all three branches of my trigeminal nerve, the fifth cranial nerve. He also mentioned other nerves were affected, particularly the facial nerve, which carries nerve fibres that control the muscles responsible for facial movement and expression. It helps control your forehead muscles, close your eyes or blink, and enables you to smile, talk and communicate through facial expressions. It also controls a muscle in the neck that allows movement in your chin and the corners of your mouth, and helps your ear respond to loud noises. I would learn much later that it also contains sensory nerve fibres and plays a key role in hearing.[1]

Seating himself directly in front of me, he expressed concern. 'Unfortunately, you might be in for a rough road ahead because people won't understand what you're experiencing. Essentially, it's not visible. You look so well,' he explained. Renowned for his expertise and compassionate patient care, he shared his extensive knowledge and understanding of the complexities of my nerve damage.

As he spoke, I tearfully exhaled, a release of breath held hostage by the unspoken burden I carried. The emotional toll of oscillating between concealing my pain from others and attempting to articulate its nuances, lifted in that moment like a veil, allowing the invisibility of my torment to be acknowledged. To be validated.

Tears welled up, not of sorrow, but of a deeply felt recognition of my struggles. Though concealed, they were understood. His comprehension of my experience, marked by three lonely years of relentless, debilitating pain and the invisible complexities of PHTN, were words I had longed to hear. It was a validation whispering, 'I see you; I feel you,' bridging the gap between isolation and connection. This was something not always found outside of the online support group I had joined earlier in my journey.

Speaking with heartfelt understanding, he explained nothing more could be done to alleviate my pain beyond what I had already attempted. Familiar as I was with such declarations, I was not immune to hearing this. However, his understanding, coupled with his offer to stay in touch if I needed someone to talk to, someone who understood, provided great comfort as I left his office.

His words, 'unfortunately people won't understand,' were words that whispered of disconnection. These words would become a catalyst for an unexpected and at times intensely painful internal transformation. For now, the disconnection felt like loss. Rejection. Abandonment. Aloneness.

As I left the surgeon's room and walked across the corridor to the endodontist, I felt comforted knowing there was someone who understood my condition and that the procedure would go ahead. As I lay back in the chair once again, the endodontist handed me a stress ball and squeezed my hand – a subtle acknowledgement of how excruciating this would be for someone with PHTN. For three painstaking hours he worked tirelessly to remove the nerves from the tooth, located near the convergence of multiple damaged nerves.

As I left the room later that day, I couldn't help but wonder what other surprises this condition had in store for me. It was hard to comprehend almost three years had passed since that fateful day in April 2016, when shingles attacked my nervous system. Shingles. A virus. An unwelcome disturbance that would change my life forever.

When I stepped outside and onto the footpath, the afternoon breeze sent shock waves through the left side of my face. Wincing, I walked on as the fiery tendrils of nerve pain continued snaking their way across my cheek. *Just get to the tram. I only have to make it to the tram.* My hand instinctively reached to soothe, but was unwilling to touch, knowing this would only increase the sensations. Tears welled. *No crying, it will only bring more pain,* I cautioned myself, feeling the mounting pressure building behind my eyes. I held my breath. *I wish John was here. I'm so tired of attending appointments on my own.*

Feeling disconnected in the absence of my family, I reminded myself there was nothing they could do to help me. Despite knowing this, I craved their presence. My husband, John, was working away. He had been employed in the mines for over 30 years, 15 of which were fly in, fly out. It was a job he loved. Before shingles, I filled the void of his absence with work, social and sporting commitments. Now, I couldn't. I longed for his comfort and the security of his loving presence, his warm embrace and ability to bring light to any situation. Just his nearness would be enough. To rest my feet on him stretched out together on our couch. The quiet moments of simply being together. *It is what it is,* I reminded myself. At 47, I had survived difficult periods before.

My 20s were a profoundly challenging time. What began with the joy of marrying John, the love of my life, soon gave way to a much darker chapter. Those years marked the start of the lonely and terrifying journey through three years of treatment for early-stage cervical cancer, and concluded with a hysterectomy at the age of 29. In the years between, I endured the heartbreak of three consecutive miscarriages, each loss leaving an indelible ache in my heart. As friends were also trying desperately to have children, I buried my sorrow in silence, denying myself the space to grieve. Although unexpected, I was blessed with the miracle of giving birth to two precious baby girls, four years apart, on either side of the miscarriages. Just 26 months after the joyous arrival of our second daughter, however, my world was shattered. At the age of 28, a mother of two, I faced the unimaginable – losing my own mother in a tragic car accident. In an instant, I became a motherless daughter. I would have given anything to see our children grow up with my own mother's love and presence in their lives.

Leaning my head against the window as I sat on the tram, I shifted my thoughts to my girls. Time spent in their company filled my soul. I wondered when I might see my eldest daughter next. Visits to see her or when she visited us were one of my most precious joys. As most mothers would, I missed her presence once she moved interstate in 2011 at just 19. Knowing it was an important stage of the transition to adulthood I proudly supported her aspiration to live her own independent life. Nevertheless, I craved for a regular drop in or shared meal.

My youngest daughter was halfway through her university degree and her bright and effervescent nature added a much-needed infusion of life into our home. She brought the outside world to me when I was largely limited to my four walls. Life had shrunk around me with barely a semblance left of what it was like prior to my outbreak of shingles.

Previously, my days had been so fulfilling. Fun and adventure were important values for John and I. We worked hard to provide our girls access to quality education while simultaneously creating time and space to see and experience the world. A world which we filled with wonderful people. How we loved entertaining and being entertained. Music festivals, concerts and attending theatre performances were some of our favourite activities. We often took weekends away outside of Adelaide and our annual trips to our family beach shack for fishing and water sport adventures was our most treasured time together. We always had a trip planned ahead within Australia or overseas. *Will I ever be able to live a full and active life again?* I wondered.

Reflecting on my formative years, I had a natural tendency to stay occupied, constantly looking for something to do. Growing up in a remote farming area demanded creativity when it came to entertaining myself. My days were filled with outdoor play and adventure, the kind of freedom only childhood can bring. My elder sister, younger brother and I, loved riding our bikes everywhere.

In front of our house, we would prod around in the dirt for hours, digging up and eating yams, a skill we were taught by local Aboriginal children we played with. Climbing the mulberry tree in the orchard was something we loved to do together. It often ended in fruit fights, leaving us stained purple and our mother shaking her head at the mess, though secretly stifling a giggle. During mouse plagues, we enjoyed poking the garden hose down their holes, filling them with water. Kneeling beside the holes, we waited eagerly for them to pop out, sodden and sluggish. A stark contrast to the care I took with pets and injured animals. Birds I found with broken legs were lovingly cared for, a matchstick taped to their leg and Weet-Bix given for food. Needless to say, few survived. Crosses on tiny graves outside of our fence added up over the years before I realised veterinary work was not my forte.

When my sister went away to board for school, I spent hours with my brother outdoors. We raced our bikes over corrugated dirt roads, carving out our own tracks to challenge ourselves. When he practised his bowling for cricket, I became the batter, standing in front of the statue of his handmade wicketkeeper, its helmet securely in place. Together, we created intricate mazes of holes in the backyard for marbles, losing ourselves for hours as we crawled around in the dirt on hands and knees. Time seemed to melt away as we played, inventing our own brand of fun. Throughout our childhood, the three of us fought at times like most siblings do and occasionally got into mischief, but we generally respected the boundaries set by our parents, guided by the ever-present knowing that rules must be followed.

Despite our seemingly carefree existence, underneath it all an emptiness lingered in me, a sense of impermanence tied to the ever-present shadow of illness. My childhood days often felt like a waiting game, anticipating the next time my lungs would fail me and another hospital stay would begin. The thoughts loomed constantly amidst an unsettling feeling I was a temporary member of my family, of not quite belonging to the tribe. Beneath it all lay a nameless fear, incomprehensible and unspoken. A quiet yet persistent undercurrent in my inner world. While it felt like a dam waiting to burst, I held it tightly in place as I occupied myself with activities.

During my childhood, I also found joy in reading novels and short stories from magazines or in my father's Readers Digest books. With an inquiring mind, books brought the world into my very remote corner of it. I would often craft my own short stories or imagine myself in the places I read about, hoping one day I might travel to them. On hot days, I spent quiet moments building a stamp collection (something I didn't entirely love but it kept me occupied). I was also drawn to various creative pursuits, like gathering wildflowers to make arrangements or learning a new craft like macrame. Whether alone or with others, my days were full, shaped by a deep desire to keep my hands occupied and my mind engaged, anything to relieve me from boredom and distract myself. I never sat idle.

When not outdoors or occupied on my own, I cherished the moments spent with my mother. Anything to be near her, to feel close to her. Her presence brought me a sense of comfort and safety, yet it was accompanied by confusing feelings of a contradictory sense of distance. At times she felt just beyond reach, as though a part of her existed in a world I couldn't access. That elusiveness stirred a deep loneliness in me, a yearning that proximity alone could never satisfy.

One of my most treasured memories is of accompanying her to evening classes held at our little school of 14 students. Local mothers gathered there to learn typing, and I felt a quiet pride being by her side learning to type with her. Those evenings together were special.

Baking with her or learning to sew under her patient guidance was similarly meaningful. They weren't just activities – they were shared moments of connecting, creativity and learning. My mother loved to sew, and her sewing machine, her most prized possession, felt like an extension of her. It was where she spent countless hours, making clothes for us or creating other beautiful pieces. She found quiet joy in her work. Sharing this love with her brought a closeness I treasured.

I'll never forget her teaching me to use her precious sewing machine. She was so patient, sitting beside me on her stool, gently guiding my small hands. She showed me how to move the fabric, follow the guides with precision and reverse the stitches just enough to secure them. The trust she placed in me to use her sewing machine filled my heart with joy. Even when it would jam, the threads knotting up under the plate repeatedly, she rarely showed irritation. Time and again, she left what she was doing to fix the problem, calmly demonstrating how to avoid it so I could continue. To her, it was always the machine's fault, never mine. Her endless patience felt like a gift.

Now, as I approached my tram stop, a familiar longing for my mother's gentle presence rose in my chest, leaving a lump in my throat. I swallowed it down, choking back the tears that memories of my beautiful mother always stirred. *No tears. Don't think about her. It's too painful.*

Stepping off the tram, I focused instead on thinking about what I could do to occupy myself until John returned home. Everything had changed. *Will things ever go back to how they were?*

2.

THE BURNOUT

*'You cannot heal what you hide.
You cannot heal what you ignore.
You cannot heal what you cover.
You cannot heal what you avoid.'*
      Josefina H. Sanders

In April 2016, shingles hit me, permanently damaging multiple nerves in my face, ear, eye and head. My world as I knew it came crashing down around me. It was like someone had removed my batteries and, in their place, inserted debilitating fatigue. If I wondered what taser guns and electric shock treatment to my head and face felt like, surely this was it.

One night, the week before the virus hit, I was completing a task in preparation for a meeting at work the following morning. My eyes weary, I wanted to go to bed. Exasperated, I shared with John, 'I'm so exhausted but I'll still be another hour yet. You go to bed.' I worked in a rewarding yet demanding role. It was increasingly encroaching on my personal time and I had been feeling guilty for working so late each night while he was home.

As I walked upstairs to my bedroom around 11 pm, I sighed outwardly. Holidays were only days away. *I'll be fine once I can rest.* Beneath the surface however, a dormant virus was silently reactivating. My body, speaking a language far more honest than words, decided it was tired of being exhausted. It had its own plan.

The following morning, I woke to a level of physical and mental fatigue I had never imagined possible. Every movement felt heavy, as though I were wading through thick mud. As I dressed, it was like watching myself in slow-motion, each action drawn out. Putting one foot in front of the other required incredible effort. Each night that week, as I lay in bed, my body seemed unable to surrender to sleep. It felt strangely wired, exhausted yet restless. Not wired in an energetic way, but with an alertness I could not describe. The duality of alertness combined with fatigue made no sense. By Tuesday, my eyes had become oddly light-sensitive. Naively, I assumed it was tiredness.

Three days later, in the early hours of Friday morning, I woke around 3 am with searing pain deep in my left eye and around my eyebrow. Throwing the quilt off, I made my way to the bathroom to examine it. Squinting, I could see what looked like three large bites around my eyelid and in my eyebrow. The whole area was red and puffy. Assuming it was spider bites, I walked back to the bedroom and checked my bed thoroughly. Nothing in sight. Frustrated and tired, I was unable to return to sleep due to the pain. The following day I felt exhausted. My eye was in agony. Little did I know, these were all warning signs. I had never felt fatigue nor pain quite like it. I could sense my body had reached its limits. *I need a holiday. I'll rest and I'll be fine,* I reminded myself. *If I can just get myself to Smoky Bay.* If anywhere was going to provide a place to rest and rejuvenate, it would be our shack. The place I fondly named, 'Little Bet', after my mother, Betty. Just two more days and I would be there. It was the place where I loved to be with John and my girls – to fish, play cards and relax together, and where time seemed to stand still.

After resting for two days, we headed off on the long drive for our annual holiday. Oblivious to what was brewing, I said to John, 'I'm not sure what's going on with this eye but it's so painful and I don't feel well at all. I'm glad I'm only sitting in the car today because I don't have energy for anything else.'

Arriving at Smoky Bay after a nine-hour drive, my eyes felt increasingly sensitive to light and my body ached all over. Our tiny unlined shack built by my grandfather in the 1960s, sat right on the beachfront in the bay. Despite the fact there was no hot water in the kitchen and only curtains for internal walls, I couldn't wait to relax there. I loved it for its simplicity and the fact it was filled with memories of my mother.

The curtains in the shack were handcrafted from preloved fabrics and offcuts. Each told a story of her resourcefulness and humble heart. Being colourblind, she likely never realised how funny the mismatched colours and materials looked, but that was just her. She was never one for materialism, always one for making do with what she had. Since her passing, I had made replacement sea-themed curtains in bright colours to reflect her joyful spirit. Their cheerfulness uplifted me now, even in my exhaustion and pain. As I drew them closed and lay down to finally rest, I felt relieved to have arrived at Little Bet, and was hopeful I could now rejuvenate and recover.

Over the next five days, my hope slowly dissipated as my face became more and more uncomfortable and disfigured. Struggling to get out of bed one morning, all I wanted to do was rest but John cheekily brought me breakfast in bed to entice me out to fish, keen to hit the water early so we could collect bait. Fishing gave John so much joy. It was his happy place. We loved fishing together and I didn't want to miss out either. I was so tired, however, I knew it would be relaxing and peaceful out on the water. I could relax on the boat. Neither he nor I had any idea of what was ahead.

As I gazed out at the glassy water, I could not shake the growing unease. *Why wasn't I feeling better? What kind of spider bite could make me feel like this? I hope I'm not unwell for the rest of our holiday.*

Little Bet was more than just a holiday place, it was my one small corner of the world where I felt a deep connection with my mother. Despite the many years since her passing, it was infused with her presence. Her crockery, her trinkets, even the handwritten instructions in cupboards, reminded us of how much she cared for this place. Her memory was embedded in every corner. I could feel her warmth and hear her laughter within these walls.

As I stood in the boat, I tried to fish but the pain increased in intensity on the left side of my face and inner ear. The fatigue was debilitating, and I had begun to lose my sense of balance. At one point I felt so dizzy and disoriented I said to John, 'I feel like I'm going to fall out of the boat.'

By lunchtime, after returning from fishing, I lay on the bed resting. My thoughts turned to my mother as my eyes wandered across the room, settling on the tiny 1960s oven that seemed to smile back at me. It reminded me of her hands, always busy preparing food with love. Little Bet was tied to cherished memories of my mother often singing or humming, the gentleness of her soft tunes ever-present as she made her famous German teacake. I always secretly longed for a middle piece that held the most crumble on top. Years later, I created my own tradition, baking apricot pie for family and friends on our holidays there. Even the thought of baking anything right now was exhausting. *This is ridiculous. I feel like I can't even get off the bed and cook.*

Growing up, there was always a sense of freedom at the shack, a timelessness that wrapped around us like a warm blanket. Days were filled with simple joys, laughing and welcoming friends and family who came and went, a tradition maintained with John and the girls. As I lay there, debilitated by the storm raging in my face, I was desperate for the stillness and peace our special place always brought me.

Unable to get comfortable, I rolled onto my back. My eyes met the ceiling that my mother and I painted together. Her laughter filled the room as she noticed my hair had brushed against the fresh paint, turning it white. The memory of her bending over, almost wetting herself with laughter, came flooding back. Often cracking herself up, moments like these were a common sight. She had cheekily covered my hair with a shower cap.

A sudden jolt pulled me back to the present. My eyes brimmed with tears at the intensity of the burning sensations in my face, now coupled with a more familiar ache, a deep longing in my chest. The heartache of her absence. That memory, like so many others, was alive in the walls of Little Bet. It wasn't just a place; it was her. *No more tears. No more thinking about Mum. I need to focus on getting well.*

As a mother, I had built my own treasure trove of memories here with my daughters. I loved watching them lose themselves in the simple pleasures of the beach – frolicking in the sand, learning to swim, building sandcastles and collecting shells. One of their favourite pastimes was to dig giant holes on the beach. In them, they would create little seats and shelves in the sand, decorating them with shells. Hearing their laughter and seeing the smiles on their faces as we took them on tube rides behind the boat was a joy. Their love for the beach, deeply embedded in their hearts, mirrored my own. It was a place of pure freedom, where time stood still, just as it had for me as a child.

As each day passed, my body worsened. Seven days after the sores appeared, there was no relief. My face now grotesquely swollen had become asymmetrical. The tightness and discomfort was unrelenting and panic set in. Nothing seemed right. It needed checking. *This can't be just a spider bite.* Maybe something else was lurking beneath the surface.

Smoky Bay

3.

THE DIAGNOSIS

'Life is happening for us, not to us.'
Tony Robbins

The following day, we made the 30-minute drive down the highway toward the hospital in Ceduna. As John dropped me off at the entrance of the newly built hospital, a shiver ran through me. Terrifying memories of the old hospital flooded back. Many lonely days and weeks had been spent there as a child. My feelings of unease grew heavier as I walked into the hospital. *This feels like something sinister.* I had never felt anything quite like it. But then, I reminded myself, nothing could knock me for long. I always bounced back.

Putting my worries aside, I focused on the task ahead – seeing the doctor and finding answers. Whatever this was, there had to be something that would 'fix' it. I clung to that hope as I walked through the doors, leaving my dread behind, if only for a moment.

The doctor immediately said the words that would change everything: 'I'm quite certain you have shingles.' I had never heard of shingles, but I laughingly replied, 'I don't know anything about shingles but I'm on holiday so I don't want it.'

It wasn't long before the humour dissipated as he began to give me the reality of the potential repercussions of shingles in the eye and face region. He also explained that antiviral medication is required within 72 hours of the first sign of shingles. Eight days along, I had well and truly passed that time. Starting the medication within this timeframe would have helped prevent complications, stopped the virus from replicating, helped me heal more quickly, and reduced the severity and duration of the pain.[2] 'Shingles in the eye area can be very dangerous,' he said, recommending I return to Adelaide as soon as possible to see an ophthalmologist.

The gravity of the situation began to sink in. I had missed the crucial timeframe in my belief I had been bitten by a spider. Leaving the hospital, I clung to the hope my eye would be okay and I would fully recover. But frustration, uncertainty and self-recrimination persisted.

My return to Adelaide was challenging as I began a multitude of medical appointments under the guidance of my wonderful GP. I was in a world of pain by this stage and the realisation it was lingering longer than we all hoped, started to cause frustration. Frustration not only at the degree of agony I was in as the nerve damage had progressed, but also because I was unable to return to work.

Two weeks had passed since arriving home and a growing fear that this torture would not end soon crept in. Rather than subsiding as would be expected, the pain was intensifying. Daily living was becoming challenging as it became increasingly unbearable and widespread. In a daze and barely able to focus on what was going on around me, I paced the house with sharp, shooting sensations piercing through my ear, eye, head and face. Every step I took, word I spoke or mouthful I ate, sent shockwaves through my ear. The breeze on my skin, sunlight, bright lights or high-pitched sounds, intensified the pain. Touching the left side of my face was impossible. Unable to moisturise, wash, or even lie on it, I struggled to comprehend what was happening. There was no escape from the torment and I held grave fears I could not survive it.

THE DIAGNOSIS

Unbearable agony brought me to my knees each day. I vomited frequently due to the level of pain I was enduring and each time I did, it sent further waves coursing through my face and head. I tried to be brave in front of my family, relieved John was a FIFO worker. His absence enabled me to crumble freely on my own as the pain assumed control. Watching him helplessly witness my daily struggle when he was home caused significant distress. I couldn't bear the thought of being a source of discomfort to him.

Early in May, unable to manage the pain any longer, I returned to my GP, desperately hoping for relief of any sort. Driven by a need to return to work, to a normal life, I was frantic to find a way to make it stop. I had been trying to do some work from home, but couldn't sustain any attempts to think clearly enough to complete even small tasks effectively. I struggled to manage my own personal care and household tasks, let alone coordinate work from afar. I feared showering in case water hit my face and washing my hair was torture. As time went on, I rarely bothered with it until John returned home and could help.

Remaining hopeful things would ease and I would return to work soon, I left the GP with a script for Lyrica, an anti-seizure medication often prescribed for nerve pain. However, after reading about some of the more common side effects on various websites (blurred vision, clumsiness, confusion, problems with memory or speech, headache and unusual drowsiness), I opted to persevere with the pain and not take the medication. I truly believed it would naturally stop in time. It didn't.

Over the next week, this silent predator intensified its grip and continued without mercy. My stamina to tolerate it was rapidly declining as each day passed. Piercing eye and ear pain were debilitating and I tried everything to distract myself from the overwhelming conclusion I could not continue to live life in a battle to survive this torment every minute of each day. These nagging thoughts consumed me, leaving me nauseous as overwhelming waves of fear coursed through my body. The image of our girls emerged in my thoughts during these moments, an unshakable anchor that left no room for doubt: I could not abandon them. I could not let them endure the anguish I knew so intimately, of navigating life motherless. For their sake, I had to keep going. I had to push through. They would not carry that same aching void.

Crying exacerbated the pain. I drew on every ounce of strength to avoid tears while trying to breathe through it. I paced the room. I tried to rest, laying, sitting or propped up, but it was incessant. I could not escape. There was no relief, but I refused to take the medication for fear the side effects would make matters worse. Dizzy and disorientated, often falling to my left or stumbling into things, I wondered how I could keep putting one foot in front of the other. I wanted it to stop, to end, in any way possible.

Unable to see a way through, suicidal thoughts and desires began consuming me by mid-May. Every hour felt like a day and every week like a month. I could not accept that shingles, a virus, could so cruelly rob me of my freedom and my health. I was rapidly losing the stamina to continue medication-free. I wanted my life to return to normal. I missed my work and my work community. I wanted to be present with my loved ones.

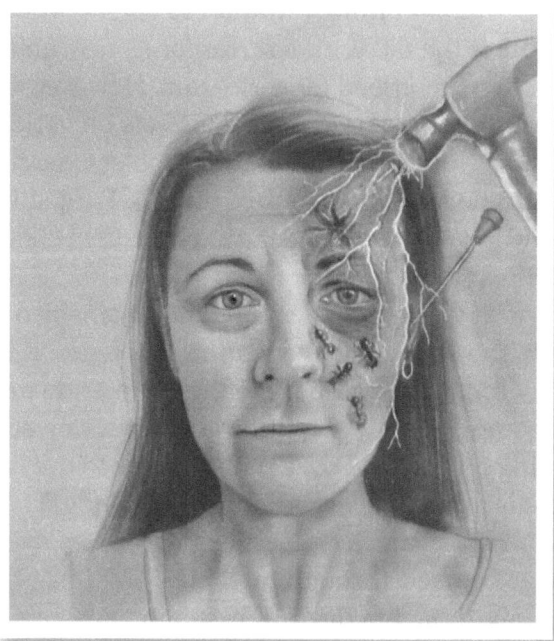

The Pain

4.

DENIAL

*'Denial is the shock absorber for the soul.
It protects us until we are equipped to cope with reality.'*
C.S. Lewis

Fearful of the thoughts I was having, I returned to my GP, not knowing what to do. Only a month into my shingles journey, the only solution I could see to end the nightmare was the irrational suggestion for someone to take my head off if the pain could not be controlled. I had chosen not to take the medication route out of fear of the side effects but I had reached the stage of knowing intervention was desperately needed. Despite the gravity of the situation, all I kept thinking about was when could I work again.

During my appointment, I shared my desire to get back to my job, but my GP gently advised I needed to focus on managing daily living first. Shattered, my reality was beginning to sink in. Walking out, I fought back tears. Sobbing all the way home, the ensuing emotions surrounding the inability to return to my workplace consumed me. I placed all hope in the Lyrica relieving my pain.

Reluctantly, I began taking the analgesics and had to accept for now the pain wasn't getting better. Within no time, the tablets slipped me into a stupor. I started on a low dose, but with it came a host of new challenges. Incredibly drowsy, I dozed on and off, resigning myself to laying on the couch for the majority of each day as severe nausea took over, along with hallucinations and debilitating headaches. Frightened, I persevered, reminding myself each day, 'If this works, life will return to normal.'

The agony did not abate and the medication put me in what felt like a vegetative state. Spending day after day on the couch, unable to watch television, read books or engage in a lot of conversation, I felt like I was losing my mind.

My ability to concentrate and process information was limited, leaving me in a constant state of confusion. I felt like my short-term memory had been robbed and I was forever losing and misplacing things throughout the day. I was unable to follow along or focus on the plot of a movie. I tried to listen intently when people called or visited but felt so exhausted from the effort of trying to take in what they were saying. In responding, I found it difficult to find words and my speech slowed down. Verbal interactions became a major challenge.

Along with communication and concentration difficulties, my hearing also changed. Every conversation sounded muffled, as if I were trying to hear under water, making it hard to decipher what people were saying. Sharp noises, even closing a car door, sent pain ripping through my ear like a lightning bolt striking an exposed nerve, raw and unprotected. I experienced difficulty distinguishing where a voice or sound was coming from or hearing what people were saying unless they were beside me on my right side. When I attempted to watch something on television, I required subtitles to better understand what was being said. My ear felt constantly full. All through the day I experienced regular stabbing assaults that sliced right through it. Eating sent pain shooting through my ear like someone striking it repeatedly with an ice pick. Gasping for breath I fell to the floor one day, sobbing silently to myself, *When*

DENIAL

will this stop? Life can't go on like this. Can I not even eat? I tried to ease the pain, firmly pressing and holding my finger in my ear repeatedly, wondering if I was damaging anything in the process.

Sleep eluded me each night with pain escalating as soon as I lay down. With so little sleep my symptoms worsened and the resulting fatigue was debilitating. Exhaustion fuelled the pain and pain fuelled the exhaustion. It was a cycle I could not break.

Having increasing difficulty with blurry vision and the feeling my eye was always dry or sticky, I returned to the ophthalmologist. I shared my concerns about the ongoing piercing eye pain and he informed me that if the pain persists longer than three months post-shingles it's called postherpetic neuralgia (PHN), meaning it is pain that remains. It had been just over two months. Recently I had been researching how long shingles pain can last and while I'd read about PHN, I struggled to accept this might be the case for me. The idea of it never going away was too difficult to process but deep down the possibility was increasingly becoming a reality. Studies revealed that for the majority, PHN resolves within a year, but for 22–46%, it can persist for 2–10 years. Others less fortunate see it remain indefinitely.[3]

I left with a script for eye drops, having learnt my eye was no longer able to lubricate itself due to the nerve damage. The cornea had also lost all feeling. I would need to use drops indefinitely to make the surface of the eye more comfortable and avoid further complications.

The situation was building into one I was having difficulty facing. I was 47. Surely this couldn't be permanent. I lived an extremely active and full life and it felt like someone had pulled the plug on me. There was no escaping the reality of it, but I refused to give up working out what else could be done.

Finding the side effects of Lyrica intolerable and ineffective, I returned to my GP in early June for further advice. The drug was making me feel completely disengaged with life and I was struggling with the new me it was creating. *How could I ever return to work in this state of mental fog?*

I was referred to a pain clinic in July and they advised me to try a similar anti-seizure medication, Gabapentin. They also recommended completing the Pain Management Network modules on the NSW Health website to learn ways to manage life with chronic pain. This was the first appointment to diagnose virus induced trigeminal neuralgia, damage to the trigeminal nerve caused by shingles. Too little sleep and severe exhaustion had caught up on me, impacting my immune system and resulting in the reactivation of the chicken pox virus.

I persisted with the Gabapentin over the coming months, though it offered little to no relief. The side effects were somewhat milder than those of Lyrica but little changed. I still felt constantly drowsy, struggled to find words, and sensed my personality slipping away under its dulling effects.

I would later learn the severe case of shingles in my face ultimately caused significant nerve damage to multiple cranial nerves. It unfortunately led to ongoing nerve pain, postherpetic trigeminal neuralgia (PHTN) and Ramsay Hunt syndrome, a complication of the shingles virus which causes facial nerve paralysis and intense ear pain.[4] In time I would discover the facial nerve, the vestibular cochlear nerve, the glossopharyngeal nerve, and all three branches of the trigeminal nerve had been impacted. In a 2014 research paper on one presenting case involving all three branches, it stated that the involvement of ophthalmic, mandibular and maxillary branches of the trigeminal nerve is extremely rare. In fact they had found no other cases like it.[5] Yet here I was, with not only all three affected, but other nerves were impacted also. It was no wonder I was battling to survive. How would anyone ever understand my pain? It was invisible under the guise of looking so well. I was lost. Frightened. Who could I turn to?

DISTRIBUTION OF CRANIAL NERVES DAMAGED

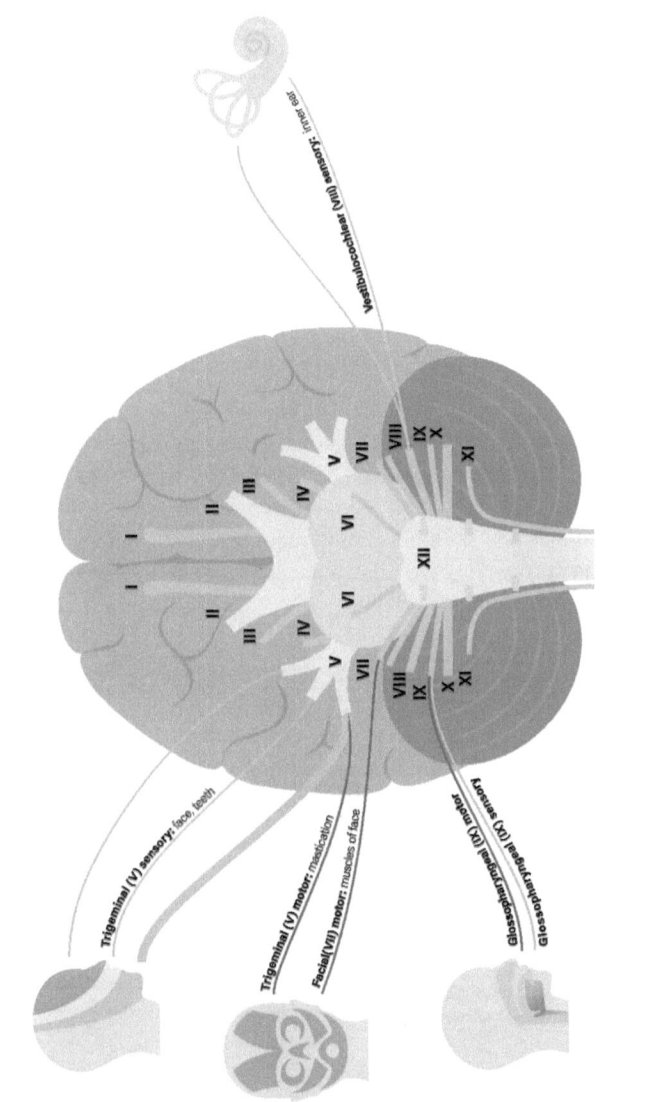

IMPACT OF THE NERVE DAMAGE

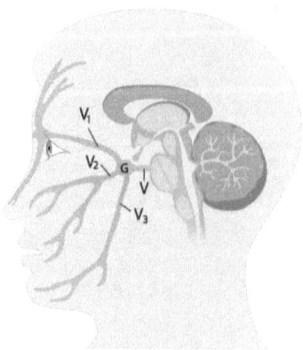

Trigeminal Nerve

The virus damaged all three branches of the trigeminal nerve – ophthalmic (V1), maxillary (V2) and mandibular (V3) nerves. This resulted in impaired sensation in my head, face, eye, ear and mouth. In some areas, it caused stabbing, burning pain; in others, numbness. It also resulted in a loss of sensation in the cornea, dry eye due to the subsequent absence of lubrication and difficulties with chewing and biting.

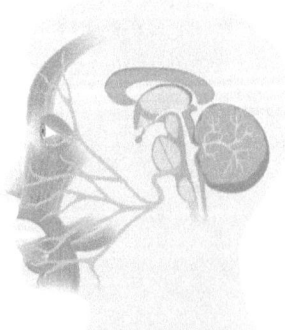

Facial Nerve

The damage to the facial nerve resulted in a loss of muscle control and difficulties with facial expressions – talking, smiling, wrinkling my nose, raising my eyebrows, eating and drinking. It also caused sensitivity to loud noises due to disruption of a muscle in my middle ear that helps regulate sound volume.

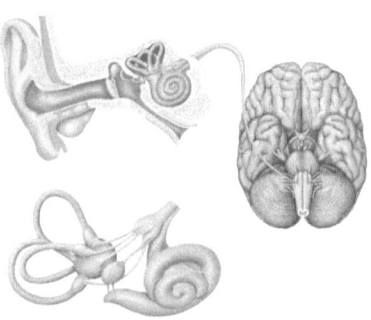

Vestibulocochlear Nerve

The damage to the vestibulocochlear nerve resulted in impairment to my balance and hearing – vertigo, dizziness, tinnitus and hearing loss.

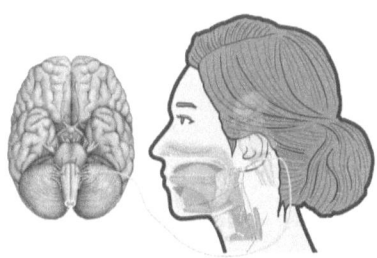

Glossopharyngeal Nerve

The damage to the glossopharyngeal nerve resulted in ear pain and swallowing difficulties.

5.

FEAR, SHAME AND REJECTION

> *'Shame is the feeling you get when you believe that you're not worthy of anyone caring about you or loving you. That you're such a bad person that you can't even blame other people for not caring about you.'*
> Brené Brown

After speaking to a close friend from interstate about my situation, she flew over to stay with me in July 2016. Having shared many challenging times together over the years, I sometimes think she knows me more than I know myself. After my mother was tragically killed, she was the first person I called. Like me, she is a *noticer* and over time I would say she became my observer friend, always perceiving slight nuances – a change in my voice, eyes or composure. She didn't simply notice though, she probed to see how I really was, her care and concern ever apparent.

In other words, she saw through me. To this day I have kept all the beautiful cards she sent. Her words of support and validation were, and still are, a constant encouragement to me. Her unyielding care and concern throughout my journey has been one of many keys to my survival.

While I was so desperate for company and help, I did not know how I could accommodate anyone staying with me. Fearing anyone seeing how much I was impacted and not wanting to be an annoyance, I found some comfort in being alone. If people saw the extent of my situation, it meant facing reality. It would highlight that I couldn't manage and needed help. It also meant I would inconvenience others. This provoked considerable discomfort.

I wasn't accustomed to asking for help, only giving it. *Did needing help mean I was failing in some way?* It certainly wasn't a feeling I sat comfortably with. I tried my best to do all I could every day to manage on my own and help push the apprehension away. I refused to stop the search for solutions.

Leaving bewildered with what she had witnessed during her stay and concerned for where this was heading, my dear friend encouraged me to let others I was close to know about my condition. As I grappled with the discomfort of this suggestion, her encouragement lingered in my mind. With a heavy heart, I drafted an email to send to close friends and family, laying out the realities of my situation. I expressed that, although little could be done, companionship and keeping life relatively normal would be a wonderful support.

Each word was carefully chosen, edited and re-edited to strike a balance between vulnerability and self-sufficiency. Pressing send felt like releasing a weight I'd long carried, yet it also unleashed a torrent of anxieties. Breathing out deeply, my stomach in knots, I felt the fear of judgement and rejection rising within me. *Would they understand? Could they handle the weight of my struggles?* My thoughts were self-critical and full of worry. After all, I wasn't exactly the life of the party.

But as replies trickled in, messages of understanding reminded me I was not alone. Many expressed gratitude for sharing the information, helping them understand my condition and daily challenges. Others simply took action and few words were required. Occasionally, some asked for more details or probed for a better understanding when they visited or called. It was a rare and complicated condition, which I would learn much later was more complex than I ever knew. Others showed less interest, triggering my fear they would not appreciate the gravity of it or they would disappear from my life because it was too difficult. Inconvenient. Burdensome.

Soon after this, a close friend initiated a tradition with a small group of us, which quickly became an eagerly anticipated routine: dining at a different pub for dinner every fortnight when John returned from the mine. Despite the challenges I faced with eating and the exhaustion from socialising, it became a highlight for me during those weeks. In their company I felt loved and supported, embraced for simply being myself, whatever that entailed on any given day.

As I eagerly anticipated opportunities to engage socially, the weeks and months ahead also brought a mounting sense of shame. There was so little I could do to actively participate in life.

I had to make significant adjustments to feel comfortable being in the presence of others. Caution was required in what I ate, or if I ate, to avoid triggering further pain or inducing vomiting due to the agony. Keeping my face still and expressionless so as not to trigger pain was a significant challenge in a social setting. Parts of my face had lost feeling and no longer moved. The loss of sensation around my bottom lip and chin meant I often dribbled, and my drinks frequently spilled out of my mouth.

Greeting people became nerve-wracking as I had to consciously offer my right cheek to avoid contact on my left side. Smiling was excruciating, but trying to suppress something so instinctive proved difficult. Consideration had to be made regarding where I could sit, in case of a breeze, fan or air vents nearby. Even a person walking past, creating a slight breeze, would send stabbing jolts through my face.

My listening stamina continued to decrease and I quickly became exhausted as I tried to maintain focus, until eventually, I couldn't. It felt like my fatigued brain had fallen asleep. I didn't know who I was anymore.

Completely overwhelmed and embarrassed on these occasions, feeling out of my depth with how to manage myself, I struggled to find effective strategies to put on a brave face and appear to be engaged. After socialising, I often found myself vomiting in pain. I learnt to adjust, limiting how much I spoke.

Returning home, I would fall into a state of delirium as the unbearable sensations in my face consumed me. *Was it worth it? Should I have stayed home?* Utterly depleted, I began to feel like my presence was not only impacting others, but my company was becoming unpalatable. Often, I sensed the discomfort of those around me. I was accustomed to being the one who made others feel comfortable, not uncomfortable. It was crushing my soul.

Socially I was losing confidence in myself, and medically, I was overwhelmed, floundering under the weight of uncontrollable pain. Reality was settling in; it was here to stay, putting my life on hold. Despite this, I clung to the hope there must be a way to alleviate it. I completed the NSW Health pain management modules and researched alternative approaches. While I was experiencing guilt at what seemed prohibitive expenditure on my health, I had no choice if I wanted to find a way to live with this. I had to try everything.

As sleep continued to elude me, my exhaustion reached new heights. Struggling with a loss of purpose and a lack of understanding from some, I was desperate to find relief from the cycle of pain and sleeplessness. I questioned how much one could endure before saying, *Enough!* Living with such torture felt insurmountable, as did coping with the perpetual state of confusion it induced.

Major issues with my memory became increasingly more challenging, impacting every aspect of daily life. Frustrated and embarrassed by my forgetfulness, I was often searching for misplaced items and retracing my steps in vain attempts to recall where I had been. It was as if my short-term memory had been swiftly erased, leaving me with a blank slate. Tearfully, I began berating myself for what felt like an unforgivable failing. *Come on, you must know where you've been? Just find a place to put things and leave them in the same spot. You need to be more organised. Think!* Relentlessly criticising myself, I believed being harsh would somehow override my memory loss and compel me to do better.

Determined to alleviate the frustration, I implemented organisational systems, placing containers strategically to ensure items had designated spots upon my return home. Despite these efforts, the cues proved ineffective. Countless times each day, I frantically searched for my phone and purse, both at home and while out. Large, brightly coloured lists were placed in the garage and kitchen, intended to serve as reminders, yet my mind seemed incapable of registering them. These misplaced items consumed a significant portion of my days, leaving me feeling increasingly overwhelmed and disoriented.

Simple tasks like filling the swimming pool became fraught with mishaps, often placing the garden hose in there to top it up only to wake the following day to an overflowing pool. Despite well-meaning suggestions from friends to set alarms as reminders, the fleeting nature of my memory made even the simplest tasks a challenge.

Though we often shared light-hearted moments about my forgetfulness, the underlying stress it caused was palpable. I felt as though I was drowning in a sea of forgotten responsibilities and lost belongings. Sharing my memory frustrations was often met with suggestions already tried and failed. 'Why don't you write a list? Just put things back in the same place.'

Deflated, I attempted to explain, 'I've tried everything, but my brain isn't working like it was.' Silence, raised eyebrows or shaking heads only deepened feelings of inadequacy and hopelessness. These frustrations caused me to shrink inside myself, consumed by shame. My heart sank further as I choked back the build-up of months of unshed tears. I wanted to release my sadness, to scream, *Can't you see I'm trying? Can't you see how hard this is?* I desperately wished for words of comfort in my time of frustration.

Confused and overwhelmed, I couldn't comprehend why I was struggling so much with my memory. My brain felt like a disorganised jigsaw puzzle that couldn't be pieced together. Feeling like I wasn't trying hard enough, I harshly berated myself further. *What's wrong with you? You need to try harder.*

Growing up, any indication you couldn't do something was often met with the expectation to try harder, to push yourself further.

My father would often say, 'There's no such thing as can't,' or 'You bods don't know what hard work is.' This would be followed by a story of backbreaking work that would put yours to shame. He immediately had me convinced I indeed had nothing to complain about and I soon developed the belief that you hadn't done enough unless someone else told you it was enough. But what *was* enough? What *was* the standard and was there a ceiling? I only knew giving up was giving in. It was failure. I never questioned it. There was a solution to every problem.

My father had high expectations of me, like his father had of him. There was a clear assumption that even if you thought you had done your best, there was always room for a little more. I grew up in a generation where hard work was respected and expected. It seemed like a measure of your character.

As a young girl, sports day was one of my favourite days in the school year. I always ran and jumped barefoot and loved the joy of flying through the air over the high jump, into the long jump pit, or running every race on offer. My long legs were no doubt a great advantage for the running and jumping events as each year I always came home with a chest full of blue ribbons.

In year 7, I was challenged in a race by a girl I enjoyed the chance to compete against each year. Running races against her were always close. Having had a successful day, we both lined up for my favourite event, the 100m sprint. Neck and neck the entire way I could hear the excited cheering from the sidelines. My heart pounded like it never had before and my lungs felt like they were going to explode. My scarred lungs, recovering from a recent bout of pneumonia, were pushed to the limit during running races. I had never before experienced such exertion. Running over the finish line, I was barely able to draw breath. Neither of us knew the result until we heard the steward call out, 'A draw!'

As we congratulated each other, I couldn't contain my excitement. I'm not sure if she felt the same way, but I distinctly remember experiencing an overwhelming sense of happiness that we shared the win. My excitement, however, was short lived. 'You should've pushed your chest out at the end. You've got to give it all you've got to finish a race,' my father said afterwards. Although he had a cheeky grin on his face, I didn't like disappointing him and the joyful feeling I had felt inside turned to shame. *I should've tried harder.* I stored his words carefully in my mind, knowing next time I would do better and make him proud. I desperately wanted to hear the words one day, *You did a good job.* To know I was meeting expectations.

At times, my father required extra hands on the farm, particularly moving livestock. Despite my best efforts at herding sheep on foot, the stubborn animals rarely cooperated, splitting in different directions or disappearing into the scrub. His frustrations made these tasks a source of stress for me. Despite this, I wanted to help him. I wanted to get it right. Make him proud.

I carry a fond memory from the holidays of year 11, when I returned home from boarding school and helped him install a new fence in one of the paddocks. The job required the fiddly task of attaching countless clips along the wire. It was a job I thought my nimble fingers were well-suited for as he had been complaining about how hard it was with his big hands. My father worked tirelessly from dawn till dusk, and I knew that working alongside him would be no different. For an entire day, I bent and clipped, bent and clipped. I meticulously placed the clips in the precise location under the watchful weight of his supervision before he eventually trusted me to do the job.

By lunchtime, my fingers throbbed. I was exhausted, but I pressed on, determined to see the task through. While my father wasn't one for verbal praise, I knew my effort had truly meant something to him. I still smile when he occasionally shares the story of me fencing with him that day.

Now, I felt as though I wasn't pleasing or meeting anyone's expectations, including my own. As my self-esteem crumbled, and my memory issues remained, I suppressed my need for comfort from others. The shame weighed heavily on me, consuming my every thought. I didn't know how to improve, and no-one seemed to have the answers. Not finding answers meant not being able to manage life in a palatable way for others, and that meant failure. I longed for a return to normality.

Helplessness and hopelessness soon turned into an overwhelming, unmanageable and all-consuming grief. It felt as though I was losing everything, including my sanity. Surely, there had to be solutions out there. Someone had to be able to help.

Sports Day 1981

6.

GRIEF AND LOSS

'There is no grief like the grief that does not speak.'
Henry Wadsworth Longfellow

By early August 2016, it became painfully evident a return to work was no longer an option. Accepting this proved gut-wrenching and marked one of the most challenging stages of my journey. At 47, I confronted the harsh truth I might be living with this indefinitely. My career had come to an end.

Feeling as though I had lost my purpose, my mental health crumbled. The losses felt overwhelming. I'd been robbed of my fulfilling work life, my source of community and belonging, along with the joy of playing sports and watching my own daughter play. My once-reliable health, and my vibrant social life was also gone. Freedom. I had lost my freedom. With so many losses, the weight of grief was like a heavy fog closing in on me, following me everywhere. I felt like I couldn't breathe. It was too much to bear all at once.

I was aware of the correlation between chronic pain and depression and had experienced depression after my mother's untimely death in my 20s. This time, I was determined to take every possible step to avoid the same outcome and work through my grief thoroughly. Back then, mental health wasn't openly discussed, leading to shame around not 'having it all together'. Combined with my ingrained beliefs about not expressing emotions or sharing struggles, it created a perilous combination. My instinctive inclination was to withdraw to protect myself.

In those difficult years after my mother's death, I experienced a multitude of responses from those around me. Some found offering empathy and support natural, while others seemed uncertain about what to say or do. Some said nothing and others avoided me altogether. As time went on, I was challenged to get over her death and move on like others do. I was even told that I had not been as supportive since losing my mother. The grief of losing her had lingered, and I carried deep shame that it continued to affect me so profoundly. My heart sank at the thought I may not have offered enough support for those I cared deeply about. It left me conflicted about my identity as a kind, caring friend. Overwhelmed by humiliation and the belief I wasn't good enough and wasn't trying hard enough, I withdrew into myself, taking the words as truth despite conflicting messages.

Having returned to full-time work, managing a young family and maintaining our home, my resources were depleted. Yet I still tried to do my best for others where I could, often to my own detriment. I felt enormous pressure to do better.

I felt ashamed of my lingering grief, for not measuring up to expectations. I soon became entangled in beliefs of being inadequate and an onslaught of negative self-talk followed in the ensuing months. To counter this, I worked harder, pushing myself to give more, yet never feeling it was enough. Boundaries became non-existent, with no limit as to what 'good enough' was. My self-esteem suffered as not only was I still deeply grieving the loss of my mother, but I had been reminded to put my own emotional needs aside.

Now, over two decades later, faced with losses affecting so many aspects of my life, I recognised the need to effectively process each one. My GP played a crucial role in connecting me with a psychologist experienced in navigating the anguish associated with the void left by the absence of work life.

The combination of multiple losses consumed me. My inner dialogue became exceptionally harsh, laden with pressure language encompassing countless 'whys,' 'what ifs,' and 'should haves'. Understandably, it became the focal point of my thoughts. My identity had been intricately tied to giving and contribution, and the inability to do so left me questioning who I was.

My situation was unfolding as a complicated and multifaceted experience, interwoven with a complex array of emotions entangled with past trauma. I would uncover deep connections with this much later. As I began working through the process of letting go, I sensed the road ahead would be extremely challenging.

Unafraid of hard work and committed to giving my all, I was determined to process each change I was facing and move on quickly. Yet, like all grief, I soon came to realise there is no predetermined timeline for its duration and time does not heal all wounds. Influenced by countless factors, grief follows its own course. That path can be painfully lengthy, despite our best efforts to navigate through it. Grief, like weeding the garden, is a messy, ongoing chore. It requires regular attention to stop it from overtaking everything else.

My inability to work, challenging to accept on its own, grew heavier with the cascading impact of ongoing health complications and living in persistent, uncontrollable pain. Regardless, it didn't stop the desperation to move forward, driven by the emptiness that had settled in its place.

Trying to navigate this complex situation amidst emotional turmoil, I realised I needed a break from the monotony. I needed to figure out my next steps and discover what purpose could look like within these challenging circumstances.

I felt adrift in every aspect of my life. Despite my body signalling the need to stop and rest, to cease constant giving, my mind resisted its call. I longed for life to return to how it had been. Forced to acknowledge I was unable to complete my working days in a teaching career I loved, one that provided purpose and the platform to do what I loved best, I felt lost. Who was I now without this role?

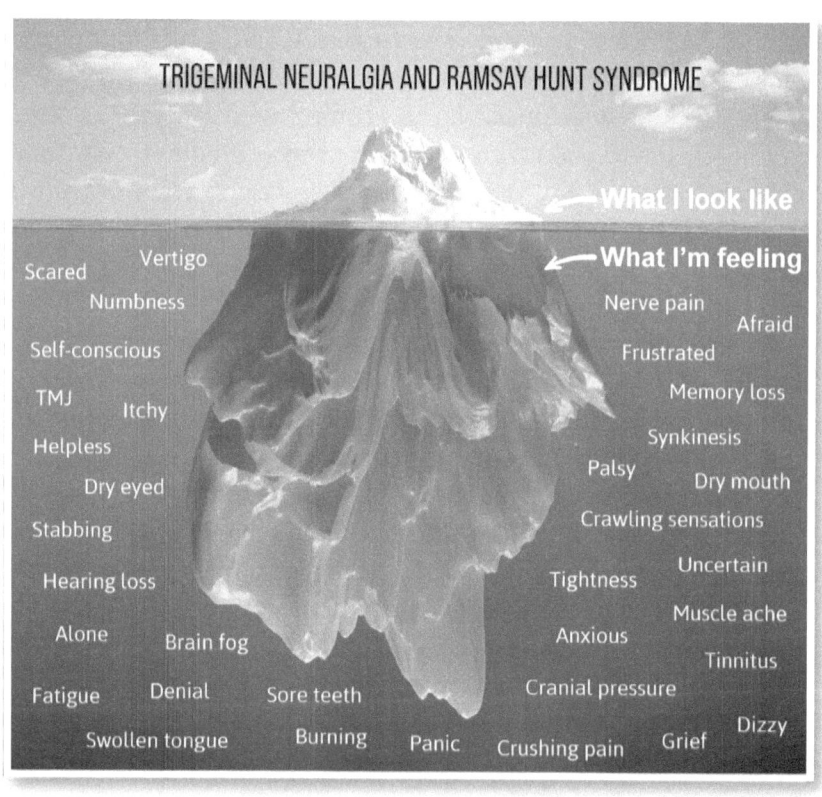

Hidden beneath the surface

7.

REALITY SLAP

'And, unfortunately, the slap is just the beginning. What comes next is much harder. For once the slap wakes us up, we then face the gap.'
Dr Russ Harris

A sense of helplessness and hopelessness pervaded our home. I struggled to cope with both the physical pain and the emotional anguish that came with accepting I would not be returning to work. Tearfully, I said to John, 'I cannot go on living like this. I've lost so much and this face pain is unbearable. I don't know how to live with it.' I wanted my life back. My desperation to escape the pain left us both overwhelmed, lost in the face of an uncertain future.

John, sensing my despair, took it upon himself to organise something special to uplift my spirits and nurture my body. He arranged for me to attend a 7-day health retreat in Queensland. Despite my concerns about managing it, the prospect of relaxation massages, warm spas and nurturing sounded like heaven. While I had to acknowledge my situation had changed indefinitely, I was at a loss to how my life could proceed. A blissful health retreat seemed like a promising place to begin.

In October 2016, we flew to Queensland and embarked on a long drive to the retreat. While a sense of solemnity lingered, a shared eagerness to focus on something positive was present. Farewelling John once we arrived, I felt overwhelming gratitude for his love and support. The retreat came with a substantial cost, and that alone motivated me to make the most out of the experience. Uncertain about what the week held for me, I committed to using this time as an opportunity to rejuvenate and reset. I sought reprieve not only for myself but also for John. He had been accustomed to arriving home from the mine site to a full and vibrant social life, filled with events connecting with loved ones. Instead, he was now met with jobs I could not attend to and helping around the home. I wanted to get well as much for him as for myself.

Exhausted and on the verge of collapse, I eagerly anticipated being freed from responsibilities and having the time to reflect while indulging in some pampering. However, the retreat turned out to be a stark contrast to the relaxing experience I envisioned. It was more of an unconventional bootcamp designed to support individuals through challenging circumstances. Unaware at the time, it was the reset I never knew I needed. It served as a kickstart to acknowledging and accepting my situation and taking a more holistic approach to my health.

Immediately, we were placed on a detox diet, eliminating sugar, dairy, grains, caffeine and alcohol. Given my struggle with eating and the loss of interest in food, these restrictions didn't phase me, until the comical night they accidentally served us bone broth with the chicken carcass in our bowls instead of the intended chicken soup. One of the participants asked apprehensively, 'Are we supposed to eat the bones?' Another replied, 'They're quite soft, so I'm just eating them.' We all sat chuckling at the situation, wondering what food would be served over the week. Most of us indicated we had no intention of consuming chicken carcass, soft or not. Fortunately, one of the workshop leaders overheard our laughter and conversation and intervened, replacing our bowls with delicious soup.

Technology was locked away, and our days consisted of early morning and evening yoga sessions, along with daily workshops covering various aspects of health. We delved into the art of meditation and the importance of regularly eliciting a relaxation response. The program included interactions with chefs, counsellors, yoga instructors, art therapists and even blood assessments with biochemists. While there was ample rest time, it was also an intense, holistic experience. I eagerly engaged in every learning opportunity. Desperate to return to good health, I recognised while I couldn't control all aspects of my condition, I could explore the potential impact of an anti-inflammatory diet on healing and pain reduction. The retreat's significant focus on gut health aligned with my goal of eating only whole foods, offering a potential avenue for improvement through diet. *Maybe if I could get my nutrition right, I could make a difference*, I thought.

On the fourth day of the retreat, I had a profoundly impactful conversation that reshaped my understanding of my condition. Finding a quiet spot by the pool to rest, I was approached by a retreat leader. Tearfully, I shared my situation. 'Do you realise what's happened?' she enquired.

'What do you mean?' I replied with confusion.

She used the analogy of a frayed electrical cord on a vacuum cleaner to explain. Initially, we might notice the plastic around the power cord splitting, but the vacuum cleaner still works so we ignore the wear and tear and keep using it. Over time, the wires become exposed, but since it's still functioning, we continue to use it. Eventually, the wires themselves fray, but we persist, until one day, they weaken and finally give way, and the vacuum stops working altogether. Staring at me intensely, she connected this analogy to my shingles outbreak, stating, 'This is what's happened to your nervous system.' Her words hit me like a freight train, and I felt a deep understanding in the pit of my stomach. My body was essentially a messenger, speaking a language far more honest than I could express in words.

The analogy was confronting. This was the only body I would get, and it was evident I needed to care for it by living life differently. The challenge was clear, but I didn't know how to make the change.

The facilitator gently took my hand and placed it over my heart, saying, 'It's time you started listening to the little girl inside of you. It's time to stop, to say yes to you, to give the little girl in you the love and attention she desperately needs instead of giving it to everyone else. It's time to make yourself a priority.'

Feeling fragile, her words sounded foreign. What did she mean by this? *Give myself love and attention? What did it look like? What did I need anyway? And who was I if I couldn't help others?* Prioritising myself sounded selfish. Tearfully, I returned to my room and journalled my reflections on my thoughtful nature. *Why would I change this?* My writing unexpectedly brought up the pain of not being supported in the past during my own times of need, despite willingly being there for others. Wrestling with a lifetime of putting others' needs first, I now faced a new challenge. How do I say no to others and yes to myself when I loved helping others? It's what I do. It's who I am. A sadness settled in me, making me feel more alone than ever.

During the retreat, one of the staff members identified that I was deeply entrenched in a fear of doing wrong, to the point where it seemed ingrained in my DNA. 'The people pleaser in you is so automatic you don't even think about it.' Confusion washed over me. I couldn't connect with it. Shaking my head defensively, I thought, *They don't know me. I'm just a considerate person who loves to help others in need. Why wouldn't people want to be like that? Isn't that a positive trait?* This challenged my identity on every level. Lacking any knowledge, belief or experience that could dispute the status quo, I wrestled with the notion that being others-focused could be seen as negative. I could acknowledge the need to manage my energy better, but my kindness and compassion for others were qualities I took pride in – non-negotiable aspects of my identity. I sensed the internal resistance and a desire to defend myself.

Throughout the week, as we delved deeper into my past, a connection to early life experiences emerged. Keeping everyone else happy and staying occupied was a pattern I had developed as a child to avoid the discomfort that came with feeling my own emotional and physical needs. Without distractions, there were too many emotions to face. I had clearly been running from them all my life, and until now, it had worked. The exposure of this truth left me feeling vulnerable. I loved busying myself in so many ways and now suddenly it was being uncovered as a survival strategy. Driven by a desire to understand myself better, I was curious about exploring this further. Simultaneously, part of me wished I could erase what I was learning about myself. However, a shift had occurred I could not ignore.

As the retreat went on, our belief systems became the focus. Exploring the thoughts that shaped what we believed about ourselves proved both enlightening and painful. Those dominating my mind reflected negative beliefs I had about myself. *I am not worthy or loveable anymore because I'm unable to support others like I once could. I am inadequate. I need to do better. I am not worthy of support.* And the list went on. The mental noise was endless, an echo I couldn't silence. Even attempting to challenge these beliefs with the question, 'Is this thought helpful?' could not release their grip. I believed my negative thoughts. If I couldn't do for others, I was no longer worthy or loveable. I would be rejected. My beliefs were truth to me and any contrary thoughts were lies – or so I thought.

As the facilitators unpacked my fears, it became abundantly clear I was unduly hard on myself and self-love was absent. My understanding only extended to awareness, which alone wasn't sufficient for remediation. Accepting these beliefs about myself were untrue wasn't coming easily. I needed to be less harsh on myself and more loving and accepting of who I was, but I had no tools or strategies to achieve this.

During the retreat, I gained profound insights through the workshops and coaching support. As the week ended, it became clear I had many changes to make and significant personal work to undertake. The revelations were only the beginning and the idea of implementing change felt overwhelmingly out of reach. *How am I going to have the energy to implement any of what I've learnt when I'm fighting to survive? Where do I even begin the process of changing what's always been?*

8.

RESPONSIBILITY

'If you own this story you get to write the ending.'
Brené Brown

As I packed my bags, preparing to depart from the retreat, a sense of overwhelm and fear crept in, mingled with a strange mix of motivation and determination. The conflicting emotions left me confused. Tears welled in my eyes as I grappled with the intense pressure to uncover a way of living within my new constraints. It had been six months since my shingles outbreak. Returning to work was no longer an option, something I didn't want to admit. Coming to terms with my circumstances and taking responsibility for my healing journey had become paramount. Despite my doubts, I was ready to start somewhere, anywhere, no matter how daunting it seemed.

Leaving the retreat, I realised maintaining the status quo was no longer an option if I truly wanted to embrace life. While I'd gained valuable insights into various aspects of health during my time there, I couldn't shake the feeling of being lost in a different way. It was as though I didn't know who I was anymore. Despite feeling fiercely determined to rebuild my life, the desire to escape my current circumstances was formidable. I had to face facts: my life had irrevocably changed, and so had I.

One of the final tasks at the retreat was to explore our Ikigai, a Japanese concept aimed at identifying what brings purpose and joy to our lives. Struggling with the fact work was no longer a feasible option, I found this task particularly confronting. My sense of purpose seemed diminished, replaced by the daily struggle to cope with my condition and prioritise my health. It was far from the fulfilling life I'd envisioned, but it was my reality. I had to find a way to accept it, at least for the time being.

Knowing my condition affected those around me, weighed heavily on me. It evoked memories of childhood guilt each time I had fallen ill with pneumonia and witnessed my mother's despair. Although desperately longing for her comforting presence during those isolated periods, I had remained silent, fearful of adding to her quiet sorrow.

The guilt I carried from childhood illness haunted me, and now, once again, I found myself at the centre of others' suffering. Faced with two choices, to end the suffering now or work tirelessly to improve the situation, I instinctively leaned towards the latter. Raised with the belief in hard work and perseverance, I saw no alternative but to push through for the sake of those around me. As I embraced this responsibility, a deeply felt sense of isolation engulfed me, like a lone fish in a vast ocean, struggling to stay afloat. Despite yearning for escape, I knew I had to summon courage. I had to wear a brave facade, and confront what lay ahead, even as every fibre of my being longed for the ocean to swallow me whole and end it all.

During my primary school years, plagued by frequent episodes of pneumonia, I had felt a constant imposition on my family. Often, I harboured a secret wish to vanish. I believed if I disappeared, I would spare my family the inconvenience I caused each time I fell ill. I had even wondered if they held the same thoughts. With each recurrent episode, I searched for evidence that I was an inconvenience. Troublesome. Not worthy of love. Always on edge, I listened to their words, I watched for signs. Each sign subconsciously reinforced the deeply embedded unhelpful beliefs that shaped, and now governed, my internal narrative.

My chest infections would strike swiftly and intensely, yet I never dared reveal the extent of my sickness. I feared being a nuisance and dreaded the prospect of being left alone in the hospital once more. It seems there was never a time in my life when I didn't harbour a deep-seated fear of being alone in solitude.

The memories of my early childhood illnesses, both from my own recollections and my parents' retellings over the years, remain etched in my mind with painful clarity. A vivid image remains of my mother's frightened face as she entered my room at night on hearing my rapid, shallow breathing each time I fell ill. My father painfully recalls the heart-wrenching experience of leaving me in the care of nursing staff. 'With a temperature of 41, they would put you straight into an ice bath as soon as you arrived. When I walked away, you would scream over and over at the top of your lungs, "Dad, don't leave me here!"' His heartache is still evident at the age of 88, as he recounts wiping away his own tears while hearing his little girl's piercing screams.

My first encounter with pneumonia occurred before I was five, however an episode when I was seven years old remains the most lucid. I still remember the fear and deep sadness emanating from my mother's anguished expression as she stood by my bedside, her hand pressed against my chest, monitoring my laboured breathing. In a panicked voice, she called out to my father, 'Noel, her breathing.' The urgency in her tone hung heavy in the air, leaving the room engulfed in a suffocating silence. Frozen in fear, my mother had seemed present to her pain, yet inaccessible to me. Disconnected. Unreachable.

'Come on, bubs,' my father said, swiftly lifting me from my bed. With his sturdy arms carrying me, we made our way to the car, my siblings trailing behind. Leaving our house in the tiny remote farming town of Nunjikompita late at night, we drove along the corrugated road towards the highway. Nervously seated in the back of our car, I felt the weight of anticipation, knowing all too well what lay ahead. The speed of the car seemed to highlight a sense of urgency.

As we travelled the 70 km towards Ceduna, the nearest town with a hospital, silence enveloped us. I kept my gaze fixed on my mother, silently pleading for her comfort and reassurance. But she remained distant, her tear-filled eyes averted from mine. Although surrounded by my family, an intense sense of loneliness and fear gripped me. *Please don't leave me Mum. Why won't you speak to me?* My mother's silence felt like a gaping void. Confusing. *I didn't try to get sick. Have I done something wrong?* Terrified, I lost control and shamefully wet myself. My lungs, already on fire with pain from the dreaded illness I'd come to learn as pneumonia, threatened to suffocate me. The looming prospect of being left alone once again, the indescribable fear my breathing might fail me while in my mother's absence, was terrifying.

On arrival, my father reminded me of the rules: be a good girl, do as the doctor says and no crying. Fearing the consequences of stepping out of line and the possibility of getting into trouble, I internalised my emotions, holding them tightly within my body. I learnt to prevent them from leaking out, to be strong and to obey without question. Following these guidelines meant I was deemed good, and as long as others were happy, I felt safe.

Scared and alone, I lay in the hospital room for two weeks, surrounded by unfamiliar machines and intravenous drips, subjected to painful injections administered in my buttock without explanation. 'If you don't cry, you can have a lolly,' the doctor promised. Lying face down, my underwear was pulled down, the thick needle inserted without another word until it was over. 'Good girl,' he said, handing me a Mintie while I bit my fist to prevent crying out. I thought I would never be able to sit again.

During my hospital stay, I felt disconnected from the world outside, alone with terrifying thoughts. *Will I leave this place or will I die here? What happens when you die?* The deaths of my parents' siblings lingered in my thoughts. I adored gazing at an old photograph of my mother and her older sister as young girls. As a little girl, I once asked, 'Mum, how did she die?' Her words remain etched in my memory. 'She got sick and couldn't breathe.' *If my*

RESPONSIBILITY

parents' sisters and brothers could die, would I die too if I couldn't breathe on my own? These frightening thoughts triggered a whirlwind of emotions, each one intensifying my fear of being alone. Yet, I learnt to bury these feelings deep within, afraid expressing them would only invite anger and reprimand. In the silence of my fear, I had clung to the hope that staying quiet would protect me from trouble and make them happy with me.

At such a tender age, I could not have comprehended the depths of pain my parents experienced from losing siblings during their own childhoods. My mother's grief was silenced at only six years of age. She was instructed never to speak about her older sister and younger brother again after they slipped away from a respiratory infection. Similarly, my father, only four years old at the time, was sent to live with his grandparents for 10 months while his parents grieved the loss of their two children – my father's two-year-old brother and nine-week-old sister. What must they have felt, helplessly watching on as their own daughter struggled to breathe? Just as they had to suppress their emotions to protect their parents, I was expected to do the same for them.

My father was a hard worker, raised with the same high expectations he placed on us. He always went out of his way to help others or contribute to the community, often arriving home just in time for dinner, only to be called upon by someone in need. Ever obliging, I never once saw him refuse anyone help. His presence at home was commanding yet reassuring, as if silently saying, *I've got things in hand*. Stories of his mechanical prowess were plentiful, particularly how he frequently came to the aid of neighbouring farmers when machinery broke down. He could turn his hand to anything, and his generous spirit ensured he was always busy. The pressure of farming life, combined with his short temper, did however create an undercurrent of tension in our home.

My mother, in contrast, was a steadfast guardian of love. She embodied a quiet strength that often spoke louder than words. Her love for me was undeniable, evident in the countless small, unspoken gestures that formed the foundation of our bond. Yet, her reserved nature left me confused during moments of vulnerability, especially when I was ill. During those times, her silence deepened, as though some part of her retreated behind an invisible veil. It was as if she stood just beyond my reach, carrying a hidden pain that her silence refused to name. There was a weight in her presence, a quiet sorrow that left me longing for her voice, her words, to fill the aching void.

After our eldest daughter was born, my mother finally shared the immense weight of her grief from losing her siblings in childhood, a pain she had carefully concealed from the outside world. 'I never got over it you know,' she admitted, her quivering voice and downturned eyes revealing the depth of her suffering. I later learnt that my mother experienced a period of select mutism after their deaths. This silence resurfaced during my frequent bouts of pneumonia and particularly stressful periods of her life, a quiet echo of her unresolved grief.

Returning home from the hospital, my re-entry into the family was uneventful. As I walked inside, making my way into our kitchen, my eyes cast glances at my parents. I craved for the comfort of their arms, for words of reassurance that never came. We were deeply loved, but affectionate moments and affirming words were not commonplace.

Life resumed as though my absence had never occurred. Perhaps it was too painful for them to acknowledge. My time in the hospital remained unspoken; no-one asked, and I didn't have the words to explain the fear and confusion I felt in their absence. I didn't have the courage to confess that, like them, I had doubted I would survive. For me, silence and illness were inseparable, fitting together like a hand in a glove.

Each day for weeks afterward, I endured the painful routine of lying over a stack of pillows while being pounded on the back, the force intended to dislodge the remaining phlegm from my lungs. Hot tears streamed silently down my face as I suffered both the physical discomfort and the distress of remaining silent. Each family member took turns, their hands differing in pressure, rhythm and intensity – each leaving their own distinct mark of pain. Occasionally, the sting of hands rapidly pounding me became too much for my little body to bear. I would bite down on my fist and hold my breath to stifle the desire to cry out, *Please stop*. At times, I did.

RESPONSIBILITY

Subsequent lengthy hospital stays due to pneumonia followed a familiar pattern, leaving me feeling increasingly isolated. Despite the recurring cycle of illness, I bravely complied with everything expected of me, suppressing my pain and enduring in silence. Hidden from view. During this period of repeat illnesses, my sensitive nature increased and my fear of doing wrong heightened. I became the *noticer*, on high alert, attuned to any slight change in body language, voice tone, posture and eye movement. Anything. I learnt to read others like a pro, always on the lookout for any signs indicating I needed to be on my best behaviour. I just wanted to feel loved and cared for.

As I sat on my bed back at the Queensland retreat, waiting for my transfer to the airport, I could sense the presence of this sensitive little girl within me, longing for love and care yet unsure how to give it to herself or ask for it. As I engaged with the idea of self-love and meeting my own needs, a surge of discomfort rippled through me. Despite trying to suppress the feeling, the tension only intensified my fear of rejection.

The desire to feel loved, supported, and understood gnawed at me. It felt risky to acknowledge, let alone admit such desires. The words remained trapped in my throat, stifled by fear and insecurity. I questioned myself, *What the heck is wrong with me? Why is it so difficult to express my needs?*

With a heavy heart, I shook off those overwhelming emotions, pushing them aside as I prepared to leave the sanctuary of the retreat. Closing the door behind me, I silently slipped into the transfer vehicle, carrying with me the weight of unspoken emotions and unresolved internal battles.

As the plane ascended, sharp, stabbing sensations shot through my ear. With each wave of torment, the enormity of the task ahead weighed heavily on me. I longed to regain a sense of normality in my life. I had been equipped with tools to enhance my wellbeing, yet the unyielding pain screamed at me, challenging my determination.

Refusing the food offered by the hostess out of fear eating would make matters worse, I leaned back in my seat and focused on my breathing as agony rippled through my face. Grasping the paper sick bag, a cold sensation washed over me, my mouth watering. *Please, not here*, I silently pleaded.

Drawing on the breathing techniques I'd learnt from our yoga instructors on retreat, I concentrated on each inhale and exhale, willing myself to find solace in the rhythm of my breath. Typically a talker, I felt guilty for ignoring the passengers next to me, however I knew engaging in conversation might exacerbate my pain.

As the plane levelled and the intensity of the pain subsided, I began to mentally outline my plans for the week ahead. Throughout the journey home, I felt a renewed sense of purpose and vitality, fuelled by the anticipation of applying the insights I'd gained into improving my health. Reflecting on the wealth of knowledge I'd acquired during my immersion in the world of health and wellness, I couldn't help but feel deeply grateful for the retreat experience.

As I envisioned the potential for positive change, I knew I had to summon courage and embrace the journey ahead with optimism and determination.

Age 7 months

RESPONSIBILITY

Home - Nunjikompita

9.

DETERMINATION

'We all have dreams. But in order to make dreams come into reality, it takes an awful lot of determination, dedication, self-discipline and effort.'
Jesse Owens

Back home, armed with a new approach to nutrition and a variety of lifestyle changes to implement, I embarked on the mission with unwavering focus. Still believing my pain was a temporary setback, I was determined to alleviate it, or at least find a way to live with it. Beneath the surface, emotional discomfort and the desire for companionship persisted, and dismissing this feeling had become increasingly difficult. While I recognised the importance of addressing emotional pain, which I habitually pushed aside, I felt starting with practical strategies like nutrition, mindfulness and yoga was already a significant undertaking.

With my usual determination, I poured my heart and soul into reclaiming my health, steadfast in my belief it would ultimately grant me the capacity to return to work. Despite hearing from multiple specialists that mine was the most severe case of PHTN they had encountered and returning to work was not currently feasible, I clung to the hope I could defy the odds. Fully committed to my goal, I left no stone unturned in making changes to improve my health. I was accustomed to giving my all, and I expected nothing less of myself.

Over the coming months, despite the relentless grip of pain, I dedicated myself tirelessly to adopting habits that would enhance my overall wellbeing. I embarked on a quest to find a yoga studio resonating with the teachings from the retreat, trialling three different options before finally settling on one. I began practising restorative yoga, explaining to the owner and instructors there might be days when I simply lay on my mat without moving. The commitment to showing up was equally as important.

The studio was 10 minutes from home in a lovely old hall with a large open space and beautiful high ceilings and windows. But the most comforting feature was the radiant wall heaters, offering a blissful warmth that eased the perpetual chill that seemed to permeate my body, regardless of the season. Each time I entered the studio, I instinctively gravitated towards a spot beneath the heaters. The aged floorboards would softly creak underfoot as I settled into a prolonged savasana pose, allowing the soothing voices of the instructors to wash over me.

Morning sessions proved beneficial, relaxing my mind and body, while the evening sessions prepared my body for restorative sleep. On Wednesday nights, I eagerly anticipated the class, knowing the relaxation it induced would facilitate a more peaceful sleep, even if fleeting.

Quiet meditative time became an essential anchor in my daily routine, especially during moments when the voice of pain threatened to drown out all else. I made it a point to begin and conclude each day with meditation, embedding a consistent ritual into my days.

Journalling every evening became another dedicated practice, accompanied by the ritual of recording at least five things I was grateful for. Each entry served as a reminder of positive moments

DETERMINATION

amidst the challenges, with a drop-in from family or friends being a guaranteed highlight. Such visits brought warmth and connection, easing the solitude.

The presence of friends, whether through visits, outings or coffee catch-ups, became a precious source of comfort. Despite not being the best company at times, I felt humbled by this support and companionship. Their willingness to spend time with me, despite my limitations, filled my heart with gratitude and reminded me of the healing power of genuine connection in navigating life's trials.

Working with naturopaths and focusing on nutrition like my life depended on it, I eliminated inflammatory foods from my diet. Regular live blood tests monitored my gut health, fuelling my belief dietary adjustments could alleviate pain and enhance my overall wellbeing. Following the principles learnt during my retreat with meticulous precision, I devoted my limited energy to the kitchen, preparing all my food and removing anything processed. Though initially sourcing predominantly organic foods was a challenge, I researched where to find authentic supplies. Supermarkets were unbearably cold for my face to bear, so I avoided them wherever possible. John gathered other necessities on his week off. Each day saw the consistent presence of bone broth, kefir and kombucha brewing, a testament to my relentless commitment to healing through nutrition. Book club friends even came on board, many making cakes to suit my diet, a humbling gesture of support I often felt guilty about.

By this stage, I had joined an online support group, the Face Pain Association Official Trigeminal Neuralgia Network, in search of additional ways to alleviate my condition. The forum was inundated with heartbreaking stories, revealing the profound suffering and despair experienced by individuals navigating similar journeys. While many shared suggestions and experiences, a predominant reliance on potent pain medications was evident. Tragically, there were accounts of lives lost to the unbearable torture, contributing to trigeminal neuralgia's grim reputation as the 'suicide disease'. For some, surgical intervention offered relief, particularly if their condition stemmed from nerve compression rather than nerve damage. Inspired by stories of dietary changes yielding positive results, I persisted with my unwavering commitment to nutrition.

Looking through my kitchen window one morning, I glanced at the glistening pool in our backyard, hoping one day I would be able to manage swimming again. I smiled inwardly at my newly planted herb garden under the windowsill. I felt an overwhelming sense of gratitude as I reflected on what John was doing to support me and my approach. I rinsed my weekly supply of organic vegetables, fresh from the market that morning, ready for a new batch of soup. As I glanced around the wide expanse of our open living area, a familiar heaviness settled in my stomach. This was my reality – alone, stuck at home trying to manage pain and nourish myself.

We had built our lovely home as we wanted it, furnishing our living area with carefully chosen pieces designed for the space, but now it was beginning to feel like a prison. Large white porcelain tiles covered the expansive area, however the tiled floors were icy cold and downstairs was always chilly.

Glancing down at dirty footprints and spots of food spillage on the kitchen floor, frustration overwhelmed me as I was reminded yet again of things I found difficult to do. Mopping and cleaning exacerbated my dizziness which triggered instant nausea. When bending and putting my head down I often lost my balance and toppled to the floor. My home reminded me constantly of what I couldn't do anymore.

Spending my days indoors to protect myself from any triggers that would increase my pain, I was beginning to feel suffocated by the monotony, the silence and the aloneness. *I can't stay in these four walls forever*, I thought. *I have to beat this thing.* Getting my food right became a full-time job. It wasn't the occupation I was looking for but I hoped it would be the answer to helping me return to a workplace one day.

While I worked tirelessly on my new lifestyle changes after the retreat, my pain had not yet abated and the pain medication continued having a detrimental impact on daily living. I wanted to find another avenue for pain management that didn't involve drugs. Despite varying accounts on the support group about the use of acupuncture to reduce pain, I began working with an

DETERMINATION

acupuncturist three or four times a week. He was a wonderful support for me holistically and drew on the knowledge of his vast network of practitioners to try different approaches for treating my condition. Vomiting after the sessions was a frequent occurrence as I walked home from my appointments. Even though the ease I felt was short-lived, it was worth it just for the breathing space it sometimes gave me for up to an hour. I would continue this demanding regime for 18 months before I determined the benefit did not outweigh the time, energy and commitment. My search for effective pain management continued.

10.

ALONENESS

'Courage doesn't always roar. Sometimes courage is the quiet voice at the end of the day saying, "I will try again tomorrow."'
Mary Anne Radmacher

In mid-November 2016, another sleepless night saw me wake at 2:30 am. The familiar ache burning deep in my temple signalled the unwelcome start to my day. My face was under siege with the regular stabbing pains that had become my consistent alarm clock, shattering the silence and robbing me of a full night's sleep.

As was customary, my left eye, feeling like it was caught in a sandstorm, remained stubbornly closed. Attempting to open it, the eyelid grated my eyeball like a cheese grater while I groped at the top of my bedside table in search of eye drops. Annoyed, I realised I had forgotten to replenish my bedside stash. The normal reflex of the eye naturally lubricating itself was yet another hidden loss, a consequence of damage inflicted on the ophthalmic nerve.

Moving slowly to sit up in bed, I reached for my phone to access the light. I'd been feeling more weary than usual over the past few days. Slowly I made my way to the bathroom, following the torchlit path from our bed to the ensuite. My balance was a significant issue in the dark, so the light was more necessary than ever to stop me falling over.

Reaching for a vial of eyedrops, I popped the cap off and tilted my head back, squeezing the liquid in. With no feeling there anymore, I felt nothing. *Did they go in?* I wondered. Bringing my head back upright, I felt the instant relief as the drops finally reached my eyes, restoring some much-needed moisture.

Wearily, I checked my phone calendar to see what appointments awaited me. *Please be just one,* I thought, my fatigue weighing heavily on me. 'Three again,' I groaned, a sinking feeling settling in my stomach. Looking in the mirror I could see the toll exhaustion had taken on me. The usual spark in my eyes was gone, replaced by a hollow emptiness.

Noticing the droop of my left eye, more prominent than usual when I was fatigued, I glanced over to compare it to my right. And then I saw them. Three small spots near my right eye, lined up in a row. My stomach lurched, panic rising. *No, surely this can't be shingles again.* It had only been seven months since the last time. *Is this even possible?*

Slowly, I made my way back to bed, crawling under the sheets beneath a cloud of hopelessness. Picking my phone up, I opened the Calm app and listened to Tamara Levitt's soothing voice on the meditations. Any heightened emotions seemed to exacerbate my pain, making it crucial to stay calm through challenges. I lay quietly, waiting for morning to come so I could see my GP once again, hoping for answers and relief.

Confirming it was shingles, my GP sent me off with a script for a batch of Famvir, the herpes zoster antiviral, to prevent the virus from progressing. With a lump in my throat and choking back sobs, I left her medical rooms and headed for the car park. Sitting in the car, I hung my head in disbelief. With a heavy heart I breathed deeply, closing my eyes as I rested my head on the steering wheel. *How much more can I take? I feel so weary. What else can I do to improve my health?* My commitment was unfailing and unquestionable, yet with all that work my body was not responding.

Calling John that evening, shame biting at my heels, I readied myself to disclose that my health had taken another dive. Trying to suppress the sadness and hopelessness I felt, I tearfully expressed my frustration after sharing my news. 'John, what am I doing wrong? I'm doing all I can to give my body what it needs. My days are filled with nothing else but food preparation and appointments and even that's too much. I can't do any less than I am. There's no joy at all in this life.'

'Oh, no,' he muttered quietly, the devastation and helplessness clear in his response. Feeling a rush of guilt, I quickly pivoted and gave him what I thought he needed to hear.

'I've got the antiviral early enough this time so that's a positive,' I voiced light-heartedly. In other words, *Don't worry, I'll be okay.*

'Well done. Hopefully that'll stop it getting as bad this time,' he said, his voice carrying a gentle tone of approval.

Trying to keep things light while he was away was important. I didn't always get it right, but I had learnt he was okay if I was okay, so I tried to minimise my sharing. Shifting our conversation, I asked about his day, eager for the distraction. He shared amusing anecdotes from the mine, a nightly ritual that never failed to lift my spirits.

Over the years, I've come to recognise John's approach to handling difficult situations. His tendency to simplify problems to minimise distress could often be frustrating yet certainly proved useful during his weeks away. One of his coping mechanisms is to deflect with humour, bringing lightness to issues – a strategy, while often amusing and well received, can also be frustrating during serious discussions. Bad dad jokes had long been a defining feature in our family home, offering both welcomed humour and occasional exasperation.

Our dynamics were intriguingly complementary. My strategy was to safeguard others' emotions, and in part my own, by not clearly expressing my needs. His inclination was avoidance. I would manage as much as possible on my own to spare him discomfort but this unintentionally contributed to a cycle of frustration, reflecting the unconscious nature of our strategies. At times, we each inadvertently aggravated the other. Despite the deep and undeniable love in our relationship, our individual avoidance strategies were unhealthy. This realisation had eluded us for some time and may have remained undiscovered had we not been faced with such a life-changing disruption.

Crawling into bed that night, I suppressed tears of sadness. Facing yet another health challenge in solitude, I acknowledged a lifelong pattern of enduring significant health struggles alone. While it had become my norm, I couldn't deny the longing for companionship during these times. I craved John's presence, his warm embrace, and the sense of safety he brought by simply being there. *With another bout of shingles to endure, was it time to say I can't do it alone anymore?*

Longing for his presence but hesitant to disrupt his life, I suppressed the desire to ask John to come home. Despite constantly reminding myself it was unfair to ask this of him, the internal struggle remained. *My health cannot stop his work life. He needs normality,* I reasoned. Yet, beneath the surface, conflicting thoughts persisted. *I can't keep fighting this alone. I'm tired of the emptiness. The isolated long stretches on my own unwell, seem never-ending. I can't even keep on top of the basics.* For a moment, my fear of solitude took over. Sharply, I pushed it aside. The recurring mantra echoed, *You need to be strong. Don't burden others. Don't make it harder on them.*

The familiar instinct to prioritise others resurfaced and I swiftly dismissed my need for emotional support through his companionship. Layering this with my desire for John to conclude his mining career on his terms, I pushed all thoughts aside. My health had already forced a halt to a career I loved, and I didn't want the same outcome for him. He had already endured enough loss, and I couldn't bear the thought of being the cause for his much-loved career coming to an end prematurely. John took immense pride in his work as a driller, his joy and sense of fulfillment evident in every story he shared about his days away. *No, I wouldn't have him relinquish his job for my sake.*

Aware of the whispers of others, 'He should be home with you,' I felt a degree of sadness each time those words were uttered. We held deep respect and understanding of each other's passion for our chosen careers, and while he knew I longed to have him home, he also felt my love and support for him continuing his work. Constantly reminding him of my internal struggle was not an option. Committing to cease FIFO work in three years, I wished to respect his plan.

Brushing aside the weight of loneliness, I hastily reassured myself I could endure the periods of temporary separation that came with FIFO work as I always had. He would be home in a week. *He doesn't need to witness any more of my distress than he has to,* I resolved. Whether at home or hearing his voice on the phone, John's presence had a comforting effect, alleviating the internal solitude that seemed to accompany my invisible pain condition.

Collecting myself, I acknowledged I wasn't entirely alone; our youngest daughter still lived at home, a source of both heartache and comfort. It hurt to know she had to see me this way, that in her early 20s she had to deal with the roller-coaster of my experience. Despite yearning for more of her presence, I also found solace in her busy life, sparing her from witnessing the entirety of my struggle. Her packed schedule of university commitments, work, sports and friendships shielded her from the full extent of my challenges. Still, as I watched her, I often worried about the unintended messages I had sent both daughters over the years through my unconscious need to fill every moment.

Her presence in the home, whether rushing between commitments or immersed in her studies, was a great distraction. I craved company, even if it was only the felt presence of another person. Yet, clearly articulating my specific needs proved challenging. When I did manage to express them, guilt and discomfort overwhelmed me. I often backtracked. This gave my family conflicting messages and left them confused, and at times, frustrated. The roots of this struggle to convey my needs would only surface later on. It was a realisation that fuelled a longing to have known about it much earlier in life.

Knowing we wouldn't have our daughter home for much longer I wanted to enjoy aspects of her life I could still be involved in for as long as I could. Over the years I loved watching our children play sport, dance or perform. Those treasured moments gave me inexplicable joy and watching her play basketball was no exception. It was a highlight in my week when I could watch our ball of energy on the court. She played with such enthusiasm and tenacity.

One night, unable to go with her as I once had, I remained on the couch knitting to distract myself from my pain. 'Good luck,' I called out, my voice carrying both encouragement and the twinge of disappointment at my inability to join her. Despite my best efforts to attend and score her games, each whistle blow amplified the agony. The sharp, piercing sensation in my ear impacted my attempts to focus and keep track of the score. During winter, the chilly air in the stadiums, intolerable for my face, also prevented me from joining her. Pained at letting her down, and pained at my own loss, I let the tears fall silently. 'Thanks Mum,' she called out, closing the door behind her. Each time she dressed in her blue and gold uniform, I couldn't help but feel the ache of sadness when she dashed out the front door alone.

Accepting that John couldn't be expected to return home, I made a conscious decision to maintain the status quo in navigating the repeat shingles attack. Still, the prospect of being alone through further complications felt undeniably daunting. The conflicting emotions of both fearing and craving company created a tumultuous inner state. But despite these emotional currents, the primary emphasis persisted: regaining my health. *I have the antiviral this time*, I reminded myself. *All I need is rest.*

11.

THE SEARCH FOR UNDERSTANDING

> *'Without experiencing that others know us, or are able to, we're left feeling alone – at times, despairingly so. It's a bleak place to be and can lead to feelings of emptiness and despondency. In such a state, we're even vulnerable to taking our lives.'*
> Psychology Today

The following morning, panic gripped me at the thought the return of this unwelcome visitor could threaten to take over both sides of my face. Alone and frightened I felt a desperate urge to cry out, *This needs to end! I've reached my limit. I want my life back!* Yet these thoughts clashed with feelings of guilt and failure, as if enduring silently was a measure of strength.

In the quiet of my own thoughts, I urged myself to persist, to keep striving. The idea of confiding in someone, of sharing the recurring urge of wanting my life to end, briefly crossed my mind. But fear held me back. *That's too much for them to carry. What if their response added to my pain? Would they judge me as weak? A failure?*

Selfish? Would they withdraw, pass judgement or abandon me if they truly grasped how desperate I felt?

After sharing openly previously, I was left feeling guilty. My friends were uncomfortable, their helplessness mirrored on their faces. Even among trusted friends with whom I could be open, the thought of articulating my current anguish felt daunting. *They just need to hear I'm okay, not that I don't think I can endure this.* Still, a persistent longing remained – for someone to truly hear me and offer comfort. To show they understood.

Walking downstairs, I stumbled, grabbing at the railing as I lost my balance after looking down. *Concentrate*, I reminded myself. Terrified of the road ahead, I acknowledged the weight of facing this alone. My body heaved. Wracked with sobs, uncontrollable tears began to fall despite my fight to suppress them. *I want to live. I don't want my life to end. I just don't know how it's possible to survive this.*

The situation was too much for anyone. I didn't want pity or sympathy. What I wanted more than ever was compassion. But without understanding, how could compassion truly manifest? And without openness, how could there be understanding?

The pervasive belief that no matter how much I tried, no-one would ever grasp what I was going through clouded my thoughts. I felt alone, uncertain where to seek support. Specialists warned me about the challenges ahead, emphasising the difficulty people might have in comprehending the invisible nature of the nerve pain when I looked so well. Their genuine concern was heartwarming but also instilled a persistent fear in me.

Despite heeding their warnings, the desire to feel understood naturally persisted. Some openly expressed feelings of helplessness in providing relief while others still seemed unable to fully grasp the extent of my difficulties, no matter how much or how little I shared. My honest responses to questions about why I couldn't do something or eat something, often elicited blank stares or deflections, leaving me uncertain how to react. Questions like, 'So what are you going to do?' or 'Why don't you do xyz?' often revealed a lack of awareness of the implications of my condition. I longed for someone to say, 'We will get through this together,' rather than 'What are *you* going to do?' Nothing *could* be done, yet some seemed fixated on suggesting solutions rather than truly hearing me. *I couldn't fix it, the medical profession couldn't fix it, so, how could they?*

Was it about understanding? Or was it about how much discomfort others could tolerate? Did my situation expose personal vulnerabilities? In truth, we were all floundering, doing our best while managing our own fears and limitations. Lost. Overwhelmed. Uncomfortable. There was nothing to guide any of us. Though clearly well-intentioned, these interactions emphasised the pitfalls of sharing, amplifying feelings of loss and hopelessness.

In my moments of vulnerability, the greatest comfort came from a listening ear and a kind heart, or simply company. The power for me was in feeling seen. To know that I mattered.

Depending on how others responded, I often portrayed myself as more able than I truly felt, partly so my company was more palatable and partly to protect myself. Even during some phone calls when cognitive fatigue set in and my pain couldn't be controlled, rather than admit I was tired, I muted myself so they couldn't hear me vomit. Still listening, I sometimes heard, 'Are you still there?' I hoped they didn't notice any change in my demeanour when I quickly unmuted myself to respond. The comforting presence of a voice on the phone took precedence over the fatigue and pain as I tried to remain present. However, I was beginning to realise pushing myself to appear okay was feeding the need for understanding even further. I was my own worst enemy.

This self-sabotaging behaviour, trying to show up with a cheery disposition, only amplified my suffering. But in truth, what else could I do? *Was there any point in advocating for myself?* I wondered. *A degree of stoicism is required, but I feel so alone.* It was a familiar experience others regularly expressed in the support group.

Once downstairs, I sat at the table and opened my journal, hoping that recording my thoughts would end my rumination. Journalling, however, highlighted that voicing my needs felt like neediness, leading me to suppress parts of myself to avoid judgement, criticism or dismissiveness. Placing my pencil down, I closed my eyes and leant my head in my hands.

My world had shrunk, consumed by survival strategies for managing pain and endless appointments. I had little to offer to a conversation. Despite my limitations, I tried my best to listen to other people's troubles. However, I struggled to offer the same level of support as before, unable to keep up with important dates or maintain deep engagement due to memory lapses and difficulty focusing. I grieved this loss of my giving nature. My identity, once proudly defined by generosity and care for others, was slipping away, leaving me feeling disconnected. I felt so inadequate. I did not want to be the token invite in their lives, but remaining connected was vital. I had to keep trying to be present.

As I closed my journal, a blanket of sadness settled over me. I came to a sudden realisation that interactions in relationships lacking understanding felt like they were losing authenticity. I didn't want to lose relationships. I had lost enough.

Releasing a heavy sigh, I admitted the ineffectiveness of masking my struggles. Caught between the fear of inconveniencing others and the loneliness of not feeling understood, I stood at a crossroad. The weight of emotional isolation felt unbearable, surpassing the physical solitude of my days at home. The specialists were right. Seeking understanding was difficult.

As I lay on the couch, contemplating my next steps, I understood the necessity of channelling my energy into proactive measures aimed at enhancing my quality of life. Despite the frightening prospect of living with my condition long term, I committed to continue finding ways I could exist alongside it.

Embracing this mindset was difficult while contending with the enduring pain that seemed to permeate every aspect of my existence. Was it even possible? But I knew dwelling in fear would only compound my suffering.

12.

ACCEPTANCE

'What is the bravest thing you ever said?' asked the boy. 'Help,' said the horse. 'Asking for help isn't giving up,' said the horse, 'it's refusing to give up.'
Charlie Mackesy

As 2016 drew to a close, I reflected on all I had put in place over the past eight months. I was again confronted by the fact my entire focus revolved around surviving and managing pain, leaving little room for excitement or moving forward. I craved more, desperate for purpose in my days. *But what was possible?*

At this time, I was offered a position to work in a facility for hearing impaired children. It would initially involve the completion of an online course. Humbled, I was deeply honoured. At first, desperate to return to work, I ignored my glaring limitations. However, I distinctly recall the profound moment of realisation that accompanied that phone call in early December, a feeling that lingered over the following 24 hours as I weighed the implications of the offer. It was a pivotal moment, one that nudged me further along the path of acceptance. I could no longer ignore that pain and fatigue were already impacting my ability to navigate daily life without taking on any additional responsibilities.

Recognising the delusion that led me to temporarily contemplate the reality of working, I choked back an overwhelming sense of despair. Suppressing tears, I sat with the numb realisation that managing a job was beyond my capacity. I had to accept the fact, for now, my working life was over. Unable to contain my emotions any longer, I collapsed on my bed, sobbing. Tears that I had held back for so long streamed down my face as I confronted the full weight of the devastation accompanying this acceptance. Acceptance that I wasn't capable of something that would have previously filled my soul and energised me. It was another layer of grief, adding to the heavy loss I felt in finally facing the reality I had been denying.

Trying to put the memory of the job offer behind me over the coming days, I gathered strength and revisited the pain management modules on the NSW Health website. I looked in detail at each important focus area: pain education, a reliable medical team, medications, physical activity, nutrition, mental health, pacing and sleep hygiene. Daily meditation and restorative yoga practices were now routine. I maintained a strict anti-inflammatory diet, fearing that any deviation might worsen my pain, knowing at every given moment I was at my limit. Recognising the influence of my thoughts, I knew I needed to prioritise working on my mindset.

Revisiting the modules helped me arrive at the crucial realisation that my pain medication was not only ineffective but also detrimental to my mental and physical wellbeing. It hindered my ability to live a fulfilling life, and the fog it cast made working an impossible feat. Given studies describe there is no intervention that reliably relieves the pain, it's little wonder I continued to struggle.[6]

I had held hope of improvement when I transitioned from Lyrica to Gabapentin, however, the overall impact on my quality of life remained unbearable. The analgesics seemed to dull my existence, yet pain remained. Recognising I couldn't continue in such a state of disengagement, I made the difficult decision to cease taking Gabapentin. The tapering off process took six months, marked by

ACCEPTANCE

debilitating withdrawal symptoms – nausea, exacerbated dizziness, headaches, fatigue, agitation and insomnia. Slowly the haze lifted when I ceased it completely.

While the delirium induced by the medication had dulled my awareness of the pain, it had also made me less aware of everyday goings on and life's nuances. I had felt completely detached from myself, my loved ones and the world around me. If life was to be worth living, regaining the ability to feel present had to be my paramount goal.

Feeling trapped, I was back where I started. More alert to the relentless pain tearing through my face, it made each day an agonising struggle. I still harboured desperate hopes something would bring an end to it. Frightened and distressed at my confronting thoughts, I bravely confided in a close friend. However, after sharing my inner turmoil, as before, I felt ashamed. I felt like a failure. I concluded this was information too difficult for others to bear moving forward. Despite living in an era where sharing and openness about mental health is encouraged, the fear of placing emotional weight on others and the dread of potential judgement seemed more unbearable than carrying it alone.

Despite my attempts at trying to live alongside PHTN, all my efforts seemed to be failing. I was losing the capacity to disguise the battle of emotional and physical pain. I couldn't see a way through. I didn't know how to make it stop and neither did anyone else. I could only see one way out. Thoughts of that single, ominous escape frightened me, however I also knew going back on the medication was not an option. Not only was it not living, I also feared the slippery slope it might take me down. In recent years, a family member of a close friend who also suffered from PHTN tragically lost her life in the rehabilitation process as she attempted to cease her dependence on pain medications. Deeply saddened by her tragic story, it inspired me to keep searching for alternative options for relief. She was only 47 at the time of her death, the same age I contracted shingles. Being robbed of life by pain stemming from a virus seemed unfathomable. Despite sensing the search for relief was futile, I desperately did not want to be another statistic.

Crumpled on the couch, staring blankly at my four walls, I felt defeated. I knew I needed help. I couldn't do this alone. Attempting to override impossible pain to appear normal, was unravelling me. Barely able to care for myself, I remained focused on the impact on others and my inability to be there for them. Frustrated with myself, I knew I needed to turn inward, but the prospect felt overwhelming.

Returning to my GP in February 2017, I conveyed my desperation. With pain medications proving ineffective and no hope for improvement, the only path forward seemed to be that of focusing on my mental health to survive the journey. A friend, with contacts in the field, suggested the idea of a pain psychologist. The notion of a psychologist specialised in this field was unfamiliar to me. My friend explained how they could aid in activity pacing, education about pain triggers, strategies for reducing medication, stress management and minimising the impact of pain on life. Grateful for her advice and support, I had nothing to lose. I simply needed to summon the energy to keep pushing forward and try everything within my power to improve my life. I discussed the idea with my GP, and with her assistance, we found a professional to support me moving forward.

13.

PACING AND DISTRACTIONS

*'You can't calm the storm, so stop trying.
Calm yourself. The storm will pass.'*
Timber Hawkeye

In early 2017, I embarked on my journey with the psychologist, aiming to deepen my understanding of pain psychology and acquire strategies to support myself in managing daily life. Diligently working on my mindset, I implemented every suggestion she provided, emphasising pacing in all my activities. I meticulously scheduled my time in an effort to avoid triggering further pain, making an effort to prioritise rest – an endeavour that proved to be my greatest challenge. Rest, while crucial, left me less able to distract myself from the pain, and it was something that did not come naturally to me. Recognising the incongruence between my exhaustive efforts to get well and the necessity to pace myself and conserve energy, I struggled with conflicting priorities. Despite my food preparation still consuming a significant amount of energy, I was unwilling to abandon my approach to nutrition. At this stage, I was well aware certain foods, particularly sugar and alcohol, heightened the nerve aggravation. Fear of exacerbating it hindered any changes to my diet.

Feeling like each day might be my last, I consciously implemented a strategy to divide my days into manageable chunks. I structured each day into four quadrants: morning, midday, afternoon and evening, with the simple goal of getting through each period. I reminded myself, 'You just need to survive this next few hours,' asking, 'What small thing can you do that will bring you joy?' With intense focus and wide-eyed determination to stay present, I began journalling my goals and achievements to stay positive, emphasising ways I could survive this. Each period became an accomplishment to live through.

Journalling proved to be one of the most helpful strategies during the more tumultuous years of my condition. Reflecting later, however, it highlighted how I had resorted to bullying myself to survive. I berated myself, becoming my harshest critic. *'You will keep going. You are better than this. You cannot give up. Just get on with it.'* At the time, I couldn't shift my inner dialogue, believing the more I pushed myself, the greater the chances of success. My words held no self-compassion. I held on to the long-standing belief that if you weren't succeeding, you weren't trying hard enough. So, I tried even harder, just to stay alive.

Engaging in knitting during this time served as a therapeutic outlet, providing a distraction for my mind. I had heard repetitive monotonous activities offered a potential strategy for managing pain and racking my brain for ideas, came up with knitting as an option. While it wasn't a hobby, I had learnt the basics in my childhood. With a bag of wool always within arm's reach on the couch, I began knitting like my life depended on it and soon discovered its effectiveness.

As time went on, a friend dropped in with a knitting bag and patterns to make beautiful blankets, adding a positive purpose to my strategy. I asked my daughter to choose one she might like and excitedly, she chose a magnificent cable knit bed blanket. Being an inexperienced knitter, I laughed. 'That's cable knit and I wouldn't have a clue how to do it. Perhaps choose something simple for my first one?' Deep down I knew I wanted to teach myself how to make that cable knit blanket, but for now, it had to wait.

I began the process of knitting special blankets to gift. Each one was knitted many times over with brain fog impacting my ability to focus, resulting in glaring errors. Sometimes a blanket would be unpicked four or five times to fix mistakes that initially went unnoticed. Despite my efforts, an error remained in each finished product, but that was okay. While they were a labour of love, they served a dual purpose of being able to reduce pain and create a gift for friends and family. For the first time I felt a glimmer of hope I could bring some joy into my life.

To shift my focus away from my health, I decided to explore another hobby I could manage that would provide a distraction. Ambitiously, and perhaps blindly, I enrolled in a short introduction to photography course early in 2017. Desperate to find purpose and have something else to occupy my day, I overlooked and underestimated all the challenges I would face.

I persevered with the course despite pain and frustrations. My memory posed significant issues and I could neither focus nor retain the new learnings. Field trips proved difficult with dizziness impacting my movements and the wind and sunlight limiting my capacity to be outdoors. Twice on the first outing I stumbled forward, falling with my camera in hand as I bent to take a photograph. *Why did you choose photography? What made you think you could do this?* I thought.

Deflated but determined, I pressed on. By the end of the course, I felt like I hadn't retained anything and, in part, had punished myself. It had been 12 months since shingles had struck. Perhaps I was still in denial about my limitations, but I knew I couldn't continue living life sitting at home, doing little else other than knitting and cooking. Despite my frustrations, I refused to give up. Without a sense of purpose, my life would spiral further downwards.

Enrolling in a follow-up course, determined to make the information stick, I pushed myself harder to learn and practise. Unfortunately, my pain worsened, my confidence diminished, and only three sessions in, I began losing hope. Nevertheless, not wanting to face giving up, I pushed through every barrier until completion. After presenting my work for assessment, I left the studio with relief flooding over me, glad the course was over. Though I was pleased to have learnt so much about photography, more importantly, the focus required in composing and selecting appropriate settings proved to be a useful distraction from pain.

Still only achieving a maximum of two to four hours of sleep each night, my fatigue remained debilitating. The little energy I had was absorbed through basic living and I wondered how I could find space for a hobby. For something 'normal'. Working with the pain psychologist, we constantly looked at ways to pace every aspect of my life, and adding something more seemed counterproductive. *How could I make life more meaningful with the little energy I had?*

While attending appointments and preparing food was exhausting, I wasn't going to risk aggravating my nerves and I remained determined to boost my immune system. Despite the time-consuming nature of my food preparation, I pressed on, at times questioning if my unwavering efforts to 'get well' hindered my progress. However, the hope for relief and the ingrained habit of giving everything my all kept me going, providing purpose to my monotonous days. Parking my photography for now, I concluded I would practise what I had learnt whenever I had the energy.

14.

PAIN AND IDENTITY

'People in chronic pain pay and pay dearly for having fun, and for having good days. So cherish anyone with chronic pain who chooses to spend their time with you. It costs them more than you can imagine.'
Chronic Pain Voices

One Saturday, early in March 2017, I was abruptly awakened at 3.30 am by the usual punishing throb penetrating deep into my ear, behind my eye and into my teeth and jaw. I lay in bed attempting to find relief through meditation. By 5:30 am, tossing and turning, I realised I was disturbing John. Silently, I gently padded to the bathroom as the sensation of impending vomiting surged through me.

Reaching its threshold, my body resorted to its own method of purging, creating a vicious cycle of agony. Disoriented and dizzy, I steadied myself against the walls as I made my way to the shower. Dizziness was an ever-present companion, a new norm I reluctantly acknowledged.

Saturday mornings had become a cherished time of the week, marked by a soul-filling tradition of meeting our friends at the

Adelaide Central Market. Exchanging stories about our week over coffee and breakfast before purchasing our groceries, the whole experience lifted my spirits. As I looked in the bathroom mirror, I grimaced at the sight of my drab, greasy hair. *I can't wash it today*, I thought to myself, feeling a twinge of shame for not being able to summon the energy or cope with the additional pain it would instigate.

Gently pulling my hair into a ponytail before I stepped into the shower, I pondered the lesser evil – the added pain from the tug on my scalp or the excruciating act of washing it. Carefully avoiding the water on my face, I exhaled deeply. With my stomach in knots, I wondered how I could be fully present at the market this morning. Yet, the need to be in the company of others tugged at me. Suppressing the urge to crumble to the floor, I fought back tears of frustration. I knew I needed a break from my four walls, but I struggled with the exhaustion that putting on a brave face brought. I wanted to do all I could to alleviate the concern and helplessness I knew my friends felt. I felt responsible for their sadness. *I just hope they have the stamina to continue being in my presence.*

Sitting at the kitchen table after showering, I was unsuccessful again in locating the grocery list from the week before. I wrote the same repetitive list in preparation for our trip to the market. Loaded with organic vegetables, no-one could question if my diet was healthy. It was full of goodness. Following the 80/20 rule I had learnt on retreat, my meals consisted of 80% greens, so grocery shopping was quite simple. The simplicity and repetitiveness fell far short of meeting my need for variety but met my new need for simple tasks requiring minimal mental load.

Closing my eyes, I breathed a reassuring sigh of relief. *Thank goodness John's home to drive. One less task to think about.* My confidence to drive was shattered after running another two red lights in the past three weeks. Air vents, bright sunlight and road vibration all sent shockwaves through my face. Driving had become enemy number one. What was once a simple task now brought zapping, piercing, stabbing pain. Constantly on high alert trying to manage triggers, my ability to concentrate was limited. Turning my head left or right seemed to disorient me and make me dizzy and my eyes tracked more slowly than they should. It made focusing on the road more difficult. Noticeably, my depth perception was off, and I found it hard to judge when to merge or how far away cars and stoplights were. Everything suddenly appeared further away than it was. The added concentration required meant driving was exhausting.

My mind wandered back to the drive home from my appointment with the pain psychologist earlier in the week, where I ran yet another red light. Thirty minutes was the longest I had driven post-shingles, and it followed a particularly emotional session around acknowledging all the grief, shock and denial. Tearfully, I had listened as she helped me work through how hard I was being on myself. She encouraged me to catch my self-talk and change the pressure language of 'should' to a kinder option of 'it's understandable'.

Driving down Henley Beach Road on my way home, I was struggling to focus. My face felt like it was the target of a lightning storm. Leaning forward and white knuckled, I gripped the steering wheel tightly, my eyes glued to the road. Horns blared as I looked up to see I had neither slowed down nor noticed the red light. Shuddering, I was engulfed by a rush of embarrassment and a deep fear of causing an accident. I knew it was the extended drive, which had required a longer period of intense concentration to focus. I was grateful most of my appointments were no more than 20 minutes away. Driving had to be kept to a minimum.

Arriving at the market that morning, I reminded myself these friends are supportive and loving, and would be happy I had made the effort to come to breakfast. The market was a bustling and lively space and the challenge to find a table formed part of the experience. After sharing warm hugs, we huddled around a small round table, scanning the space for spare seats to add. Settled in, the first round of coffees was ordered. Friendly banter about who was paying was another ritual.

As we sat down, they made no fuss, but asked with genuine care, 'Is this spot okay for you? How has your face been this week?' In truth, no spot was 'good', but some were certainly worse than others. I didn't pretend it was wonderful but I also knew the full details were not necessary or easy to hear. I had learnt acknowledging my reality was important but I still held back from sharing the extent of it. *What could they say or do even if I told all?* I also didn't like to make our valuable time together morbid. 'It's been a bit tricky this week,' I replied.

As they ordered their breakfast at Lucia's, I walked off to order my usual vegetable juice, grateful for a short break from talking and listening. I struggled to hear and every facial movement caused pain, whether it was talking, smiling, frowning, laughing or crying. While this was easy to manage at home, it was challenging in social situations. Apart from holding a bland expression a lot of the time, I tried to keep my conversations short and not ask too many questions. Besides, one small interruption in my speaking would see me lose track immediately, unable to recall the conversation.

In truth, communication was a nightmare. Besides causing pain when my face moved, word-finding difficulties were mentally exhausting and listening fatigued me as I tried to take on what was being said. I learnt to nod and respond with a word or two to avoid the shame of not being fully present. This caused deep sadness as I had always been acknowledged for being an engaged, responsive listener.

After making my selections at the juice counter, I stood back, reflecting on all the changes I had made to what I consumed in an attempt to reduce my pain. Chewing had become an increasingly painful and exhausting chore and my stamina for chewing and swallowing had rapidly decreased. Eating was laboriously slow, as my tired facial muscles tried to navigate the food before swallowing. The swallowing action increasingly failed me as these muscles also tired. Shamefully, I either choked or the food came back up with no warning. If I wasn't vomiting from the increase in pain eating triggered, it was because my swallowing muscles failed. With socialising often occurring around food, I began to feel self-conscious and fearful about eating in public, not knowing when it would happen. When out, I did my best to choose softer more palatable foods to hopefully avoid embarrassment when food couldn't go down.

Gradually I had moved to a relatively liquid diet at home, liquifying meals as much as possible to reduce movement in my face and jaw, eliminating the burden of chewing. Having lost sensation from a portion of my lip and chin, I constantly bit the inside of my lip. Lumps from the bites, now permanent, were painful as it happened time and again. Eating ceased to be enjoyable; it had become merely a necessity.

Returning to the table, juice in hand, I felt self-conscious I wasn't 'eating' a meal, but drinking it. I happily answered questions about what was in it and deflected any questions asking if that was all I was having for breakfast. Juice was often more than I could manage but wanting to feel relatively normal, it was the best option, and drinking from a straw eliminated dribbling.

At the time, I was unaware of the degree that palsy and weakened facial muscles had contributed to the loss of chewing function and dribbling. All I knew was I had rapidly lost 15kg from the little I could eat or keep down.

I would learn six years later that the facial muscles required for chewing and swallowing had atrophied. In my efforts to avoid discomfort, I had essentially 'quarantined' the left side of my face. The resulting loss of muscle tone led to tightness, which caused more pain. With the damaged nerves trying to do all the heavy lifting and little to no support from the weakened muscles, I also developed jaw dysfunction (TMJ). My ability to enunciate some words changed, as the reduced range of facial movement affected how I formed sounds and projected my voice. With the left side of my tongue feeling enormous in my mouth, I had to find other ways to position it to produce some sounds and words. Working with a speech pathologist later in my journey helped me understand how to address the speech issues. Unfortunately, every exercise we worked on triggered the silent but intense war raging beneath the surface. Eventually, we stopped. Progress was not possible until my pain was under better control.

Unsurprisingly, with the physical and mental challenges eating and communicating posed, I continued to lose more and more confidence being around others. At times people commented about me looking serious, or not engaging and asking questions – perhaps an understandable response considering I had always been naturally smiley and engaging.

Increasingly, I felt disconnected. With a face often immobile and expressionless, I couldn't always show my emotions or interest through facial cues. It had always been such a natural and meaningful way of connecting. Many times, when something made me laugh, I tried to stifle it to keep my face still. Without facial expressions to show my emotional response, I sensed at times it changed how I was perceived. My internal world and external expressions were often not congruent and over time this had a significant impact on my identity. The way I presented myself did not reflect who I was. I desperately wanted to feel normal when socialising yet I felt far from it.

Farewelling our friends cheerfully at the market that morning, my heart was full of gratitude for their company and understanding. A break in the monotony of my week at home was a welcome distraction from all I had lost. Humbled by their kindness and care, I wanted to keep showing up as positively as I could despite my confidence waning. My friendships were important to me and I knew their presence was pivotal to my survival.

As we exited the busy market, leaving the city centre for the short drive home, the internal struggle of my fear of abandonment crept in as I worried about the long-term consequences to relationships. I was making so many adjustments to be as present as I could, but it was taking a heavy toll. I often found it difficult to maintain composure. Tears welled in my eyes and hiding my pain from John, I turned my head to gaze out the car window. As I reflected on my sudden change in emotions, I realised that in the company of others, my mood lifted significantly. It distracted me from my reality. I wanted to protect that. Sometimes I wished I could sit with friends and family and let my tears flow with ease, pouring my heart out at the incomprehensible physical and mental anguish I felt at the injustice of my condition. I wanted to scream from the rooftops, *Why is this happening to me? Please make it stop!* Breathing in deeply as I felt John's hand on my leg, I forced myself to try and swallow the lump in my throat. 'Are you okay?' he asked.

'I'm fine. My face is cranky and I'm tired, that's all.' I pushed away the desire to share my emotional pain. Realising not everyone is comfortable with vulnerability, I wondered how anyone could ever comprehend my turmoil. Few asked about the emotional impact. *If they did, how comfortable was I in answering honestly – and how comfortable were they hearing it?*

15.

ROCK BOTTOM

'We don't talk enough about grief and loss with chronic illness/disability. The loss of your health, the life that could've been, control over your body, certain opportunities, financial security, people who don't understand. It's a continual feeling, not something you just get over.'
The Chronic Notebook

Struggling to see a way through, I decided to take up an offer from friends in Brisbane who had long been encouraging me to visit them. Filled with apprehension, I questioned how I would manage the trip knowing I would have to relinquish some of my coping strategies. Being with others would be positive, but equally challenging for managing the ever-present fire in my nerves. However, my mental health was in tatters and I acknowledged I needed a shift. Comforted by their encouragement, I headed off looking forward to a change in scenery.

While the cabin pressure during take-off and landing triggered a cruel reminder of what I couldn't leave behind, the comfort of seeing my friends softened its edges. During the day while they worked, I spent time taking photos in the nearby gardens between rests, practising what I had learnt. Spending time behind the camera had become an unexpected therapeutic tool in managing pain. Focusing on compositional elements and the right settings, my pain dampened throughout the process of capturing a thoughtful image.

During this contemplative period in Brisbane, I had time to reflect on where I was at. I realised how shattered my sense of belonging was after being stuck at home, no longer part of a workplace or a place of contribution. Feelings of hopelessness had spiralled with the confronting realisation I had exhausted medical options for relief. Lost in my thoughts with questions lacking answers, I was stuck. *What sort of life do I have ahead of me? Without a purpose, and enduring a hidden torment I didn't think was humanly possible to survive, what reason is there to keep going?* I had no idea how to proceed into the next phase. I had exhausted myself looking for answers. I knew it was down to me to work out how to live life with PHTN as my companion, but I had no idea how that could look. Comforted to be with close friends while I processed my thoughts, I felt deep gratitude for the safe space they provided.

Walking outdoors onto their balcony, I reflected on the increased pressure I felt to show up better. I looked so well yet my suffering was largely invisible. Just this week I faced comparisons in how others deal with health conditions and an observation that implied I hadn't been as supportive as I once was. Overwhelmed with feelings of inadequacy, the heaviness of the shame and guilt that had built up over the past months consumed me. Despite reading so many reports describing trigeminal neuralgia as the most excruciating pain known to mankind, its invisibility hid my reality.[7] Every day felt like a fight for my life. Reading how others in the support group struggled to stay alive, or chose not to, I knew I was beating the odds just showing up each day. Yet the pressure to suffer in silence and get on with life felt immense.

I had long recognised the impact my condition had on those I loved, but the comment this week was triggering. It sent my deeply ingrained belief system into overdrive as my inner dialogue reiterated my greatest fears. *You're not doing enough. You need to do better. Sharing your pain and suffering will make it hard for others.* I didn't have the capacity or ability to be everything to everyone anymore. I was trying and failing. Exhausted. Mentally drained. Spent. Yet I needed to do better. I wanted to do better.

As I gazed across the horizon, I felt truly lost. I didn't know where to turn or what to do. Returning to Adelaide meant facing reality. *If I'm only causing pain for others, why am I trying so hard to hang on? Is it worth the anguish it's causing myself and those around me?* Immediately, my thoughts went back to the period after the tragic death of my mother. Weighed down by the memory of not being present to others during that period, I instantly thought, *I can't lose relationships now on top of everything else.* I needed to push my feelings aside. I wanted my grief to vanish. To shrink. I wanted to hurry it along. But stubbornly, as it had in the past, it held a vice-like grip on me.

After my mother was killed, I fell into a lingering period of grief and depression. I struggled to be as present with family and friends, but I did my best to show up and hide my sorrow. I was only 28, and our girls were six and two years old, a critical timeframe in which to have emotionally present parents. Despite trying to source appropriate support in and around our remote outback location, access to qualified and suitable professionals was either limited or not available. To say I lost part of myself after my mother's death would be an understatement.

Despite my best efforts, the guilt and shame of my perceived inadequacies after her passing has haunted me relentlessly over the years. This internal struggle often felt more than I could bear, as I harshly criticised and judged myself, perpetuating a cycle of negative beliefs. I questioned whether I had failed as a mother during that challenging time. These doubts gnawed at me, casting a shadow over my confidence as a parent and fuelling feelings of inadequacy. The significance of the loss of my mother on top of an unhealed childhood abandonment wound would later reveal itself in my trauma healing work. It would provide the answers to the prolonged nature of my grief.

Now, I faced a different sort of grief and pain, their combined weight overwhelming me. Back in 1997, during that tumultuous period, I hadn't allowed myself any concession for my deeply emotional experience. And now, confronted with a similar storm of emotions, I was subjecting myself to the same harsh, self-critical pressure.

Having to push my feelings aside in troubled times was not new to me. Over the years my father often shared heartbreaking stories of trips to the hospital through my bouts of pneumonia. He recounted the reminders I was given when left at hospital as a child. 'You mustn't cry. It makes it too hard on everyone.' I remember the sickening dread in the pit of my stomach when they left me and although I felt the emotions coursing through my body at the time, I did as I was told and silenced them. I was too frightened not to conform. It was no different years later after my mother's death. Etched in my memory, I vividly recall the moment of hearing the news and the traumatic events that followed.

On that fateful afternoon, I had been selling raffle tickets with a friend to help raise funds for a disability ramp. John struggled to locate me but eventually found me walking down our street between door-knocking houses. Flagging me down, he asked me to get in the car, his face betraying an expression of distress. 'What's wrong?' I asked in panic. 'Just hop in the car,' he replied quietly. 'What's wrong?' I repeated as I scanned the back of the car. 'Where are the girls? What's happened?' Panic rising, I pleaded to know what was going on. 'It's your mum. There's been a car accident. She's dead,' he quietly said, his face filled with anguish as he shared the news. 'No!' I cried. 'No!' Stepping back from the car I screamed, 'No! This can't be right. Not my mum. Not my mum.' I grabbed at my hair, shock taking over as I collapsed in the middle of the road. Opening the car door, tears in his eyes, John battled his own emotions as he tried to hold me. I sat crumpled in a heap, sobbing. Shaking my head in disbelief, my eyes pleaded with John it wasn't true. Having lost all muscle strength, he pulled me to my feet, leaning me against him as he helped me into the car. I felt like I had somehow left my body. Through tears and despair I had no words for, I asked, 'Where are the girls?' He had left them with a friend. Overwhelmed, I sobbed uncontrollably. *How can this be happening?* Taking me home, he drove off to collect the girls. Immediately I was overcome with the intensity of being on my own with my pain. Distraught, I called my friend in Perth, her voice a comfort to me.

Trying to keep my emotions in check for our beautiful girls, I shared the news of their granny when they arrived home. Nothing had ever prepared me to deliver such news, let alone receive it. Our youngest was too little to understand, but our eldest looked at me through sad eyes, quietly crying as I held her close. She adored my mother. Unable to come to terms with the news, I later sat on the floor in our shower cubicle for what seemed like hours, water running over me as my tears flooded endlessly. My mind raced to recall her, to see her, to feel her. To see her quietly playing and dancing with her granddaughters. Now, she was gone. There was no place for that news to go.

John drove me to the doctor's surgery where a close friend worked. Unable to contain my distress, I collapsed against her on arrival. Holding me, her calm compassionate voice tried to console me, but the ache of losing my mother was so unbearable I couldn't be consoled. With tear-filled eyes, I sensed she felt my pain. My mother and I had strengthened our bond over the past few years, speaking almost every day. We shared stories of motherhood and had created a new bond as both friends and mothers. Losing this relationship felt brutal. Incomprehensible.

We departed from our home in Roxby Downs early the next morning, heading straight to the Lyell McEwen Hospital in Adelaide to be with my father. Entering his hospital room, I saw him lying in bed, his face etched with pain from both the physical agony of multiple cracked ribs and the deep emotional anguish of loss. My heart broke for him. As I approached him, my cheeks lined with tears, he lifted his hand before I could speak and instructed, 'Do not cry. I can't handle it. You have a funeral you need to arrange.'

His words hit me like an icy blast, stopping me in my tracks. Suppressing my tears, I felt a profound emptiness engulf me as I realised I had a task to fulfil. Feeling my eyes glaze over, I pushed aside the urge to offer comfort and to be comforted in return, forcing myself to focus on what needed to be done.

Suppressing my grief, I shut down my emotions to focus on the daunting task of arranging my mother's funeral. Witnessing my father's torment, I understood he had lost the love of his life and he needed me to be his pillar of strength. Reluctant to disappoint him, I buried my sorrow. This wasn't a moment for me to confront my own anguish; it was a time to offer unwavering support to my father. Feeling disconnected and alone, isolated in my grief, I robotically proceeded to do what was asked of me.

In a haze, I spent the coming days warding off journalists waiting outside hospital rooms or on the phone. I contacted funeral directors, prepared the eulogy, organised flowers, selected clothes to prepare my mother, and faced the many unexpected decisions that come with planning a funeral. Maintaining my composure as requested, I took care of matters and checked in on family members. With everyone on their own grief journey and a job to be done, there was no space for my heartache.

On returning home after the funeral, I continued to offer love and support to my family from afar while we all wrestled with our sense of loss. But eventually, I crumbled. Suffocating alone in my pain, I collapsed under the weight of suppressed grief. Grief I had to shut down, grief I couldn't share, grief that had nowhere to go. Pushed down so deep, it festered, manifesting over time in deep depression.

The sound of a door closing brought me back to the present as I realised my friend had returned from work. Barefoot, I exhaled deeply and stepped inside, carrying with me the weight of expectations. After hearing about her day, I opened up about the challenges of living with an invisible condition. She listened intently, responding with compassion as I shared the intense pressure I felt. Even after two decades, the unwritten rules remained; to keep grief private, protect others' emotions and suppress my own. To be stoic.

Despite understanding that suppressing my emotions had only deepened my struggles in the past, I couldn't shake the belief that sharing too much would overwhelm others. Caught in the cycle of grief, having lost so much already, I was battling to survive. Yet

I felt an unrelenting need to be stronger, to show up better than I had. *How do I get this right*, I thought. *How can I do and be more when I'm barely functioning?*

The night before I returned to Adelaide, my efforts to find sleep were unsuccessful, prompting me to sit up and journal my thoughts. Although I endeavoured to protect others, I acknowledged, in moments of desperation, I had also been too exposed, too raw. The weight of that was heaviest when I thought of my daughter living at home, who had witnessed more than any child should. The knowledge that she had seen and heard her mother unravel filled me with both heartbreak and shame.

Despite focusing on positive self-talk, my internal critic amplified with a voice much louder than my physical pain. Again, I questioned the sustainability of merely trying to stay alive to endure pain. *Was this truly living, or simply prolonging suffering for myself and those around me?* With the little I could contribute, I felt useless.

My thoughts oscillated between guilt and pain. I didn't want my friends and family impacted, but they were and that hurt. It hurt because I was trying so hard, yet it wasn't enough. It hurt because at times I felt so misunderstood. It hurt because I was gripped by a sense of disconnection. It hurt because I just needed gentleness; to feel loved and nurtured.

Desperate to find solutions, I was still attending six or more appointments each week, trying everything, at times to my own detriment. There was no end point. No relief in sight. It was a frightening, all-consuming and debilitating existence, invisible to the world. Physically and mentally, I did not feel I had capacity to increase my efforts. I was still vomiting most days and major memory issues continued to impact my functioning. Constantly fatigued, I struggled to manage daily self-care. Yet, I was pushing through all of this to do my best to build a life.

Despite these challenges, I tried to hold it all together. As these thoughts came to mind of all I battled and how prepared I was to keep going, I questioned myself. *Was I still doing what made me sick in the first place – putting in more than I had to give? Will I ever learn?*

BUT YOU LOOK SO WELL

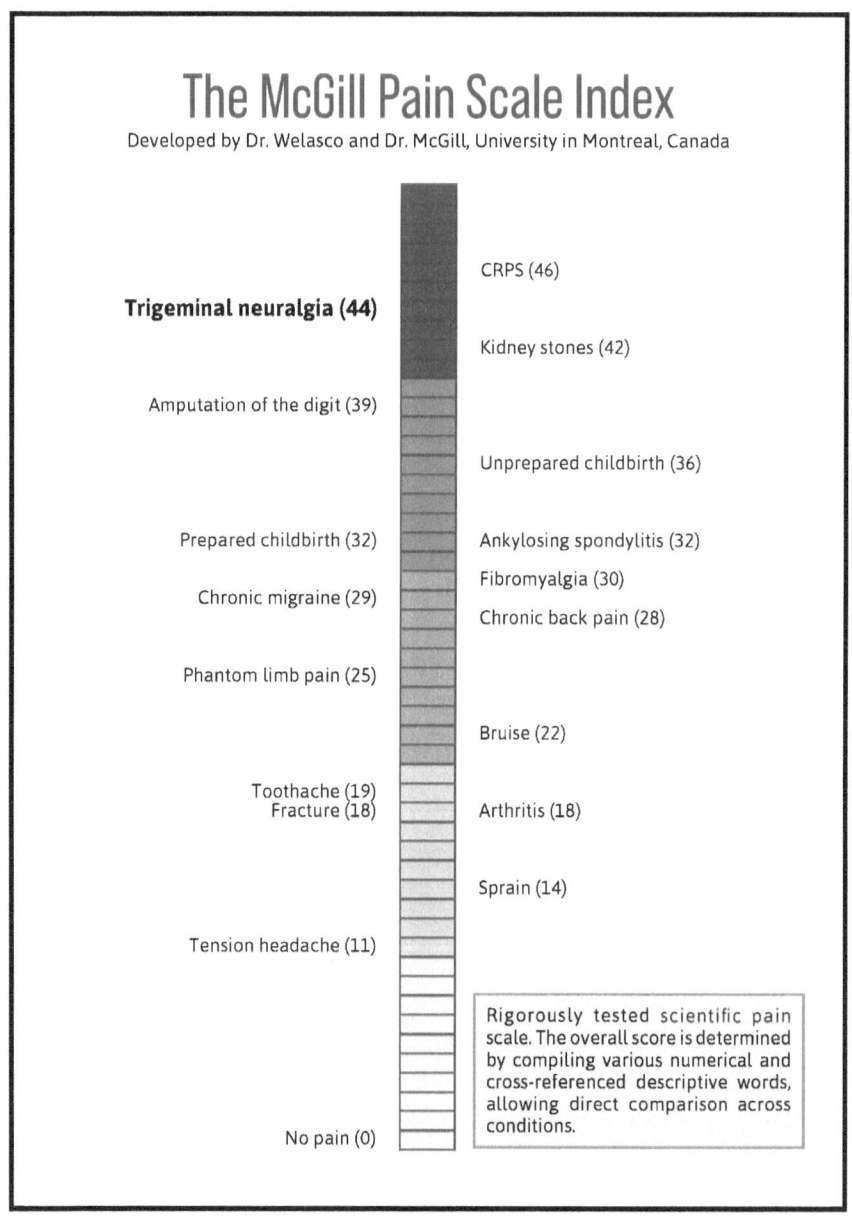

A standardised pain assessment used by healthcare professionals to comprehensively evaluate the quality and intensity of a person's pain experience

16.

BLIND HOPE

'If you lose hope, somehow you lose the vitality that keeps life moving, you lose that courage to be, that quality that helps you go on in spite of it all. And so today I still have a dream.'
Martin Luther King Jr

Desperation for a return to something familiar intensified in the months following my return from Brisbane. I doubled down on my efforts to push through and maintain a semblance of normalcy and made a conscious choice to downplay the severity of my situation.

Managing my condition silently became an all-encompassing focus, a relentless force that infiltrated every aspect of my life. I felt like a prisoner to my condition. Sadly, with my world revolving solely around my health, I had little to contribute. Conversations soon became a challenge and I struggled to pick up the phone to call anyone. Authentic connections in some relationships dwindled further, as attempts to bridge the gap by seeking understanding had proved futile. Desperate not to lose connection, I concealed as much as I could, hoping that soon I could share good news. Silently I endured the quiet suffering, leaving an aching void I yearned to fill as I too denied validating and acknowledging my own reality.

There were times I felt so alone that everything seemed too much to bear, both physically and emotionally. One day, exasperated and overwhelmed, I cried out to my family, 'Doesn't anyone understand? I need support. What am I fighting for?' The moment the words escaped, guilt – my ever-present companion – settled in. My family *were* my reason for living. I longed for their nearness, for their loving arms and comforting words of encouragement. They were my lighthouse in my darkest moments. As long as I knew they were there, I could keep pushing through. Ashamedly, in those desperate moments, I read their absence as a lack of love. I would later learn how my deeply rooted abandonment and rejection wounds had led me to think that if they weren't there, they didn't care. I was wrong – profoundly so. In their early 20s, our daughters were just beginning to find their footing in adult life. How could I expect them to navigate my situation when I couldn't work out how to myself?

The more I tried to hide, the stronger my eagerness to reintegrate into the workforce grew. I yearned to find something to fill my days, something tangible to share in conversations – a lifeline to authenticity amid the unyielding weight of my daily struggles. Despite the stark reality that working while in my current circumstance seemed impossible, an unabating self-talk convinced me otherwise. *Find something manageable, discover a new purpose. You know how to push through,* echoed in my mind. Knowing there was no pain relief in sight, I knew I had to navigate life without it. Shifting my focus away from my condition became imperative.

The internal dialogue persisted, urging me to push through all that plagued me. I ignored the endless list of daily frustrations, and decided to redirect my attention toward something meaningful. Nothing mattered more than the pursuit of that elusive purpose, something to anchor my existence beyond the confines of my health struggles.

Having recently been back to my GP to trial what would be yet another unsuccessful analgesic, the idea of consulting a vocational counsellor emerged. It was a beacon of hope for the future, when hopefully, things improved. I had no clear picture of what I could manage moving forward, but in my desperation, I craved something to look forward to. The urgency of my situation drowned out any doubtfulness daring to challenge my goal.

As the idea of seeking job possibilities through the lens of limitations took shape, a sense of unease gripped me. *What am I doing? What if I secure a job and find it beyond me? How will I conceal my pain, the vomiting, the dizziness and the memory issues during prolonged interactions?* I cursed at my condition.

The mounting dis-ease overwhelmed me as I faced a world of uncertainties, the fog of an unknown future clouding my ability to think clearly. I acknowledged the need for help in navigating the complexities of returning to the workforce in my situation. My restrictions crushed every idea I conceived. *Surely there's something I'm capable of?* I thought.

Engaging in a conversation with a career advisor over the phone, I shared my predicament and some of the challenges I faced. However, my eagerness to find a way to contribute held me back from fully disclosing my limitations. He responded compassionately to my myriad questions, offering glimmers of hope. 'We'll go through your work history, explore different industries where your skills could be transferred, and create a list of options for you to choose from. We can even consider retraining options that might interest you,' he explained.

Instantly, my mood lifted as the idea of the auditory verbal therapy course, essential for working with children with a hearing impairment, crossed my mind. His encouraging words sparked a sense of excitement I hadn't felt in a long time. Offering to assist me with an updated resume, we set a date for him to meet me at home.

Late in June, the day the careers counsellor was scheduled to arrive, the chill of our home early in the morning had already heightened my nerve pain. The wintry weather, both a painful trigger and a confining force, kept me indoors. But even inside, the temperature in the house posed its own challenge. As I gazed into the mirror after a long, hot shower, I stood looking at an unrecognisable version of myself. Pain and discomfort stared back at me. The eyebrow region, perpetually swollen and agitated from the cold winter air, displayed a stark asymmetry, the left eyelid hanging loosely.

Taking a deep breath, I closed my eyes and thought, *How will I get through winter? I've got months of this ahead.* Suppressing the emotions stirred by the sickening realisation of being alone and cooped up in my home for months, I braced myself for the chill of downstairs. If only I could warm our home without air movement.

Glancing around our living room, it appeared devoid of life. The space mirrored the emptiness I felt inside. The starkness reminded me that my life lacked meaning, a hollow cycle of going through the motions. My days were reduced to staying calm, keeping my face still, knitting to temper the pain, pacing the room, and mindfully guiding myself through the waves of agony. Each moment was deliberately planned to help me endure.

Amid emptiness, I consciously redirected my focus, searching for and embracing small moments of joy – the distant yet reassuring sound of my daughter upstairs, my friend's voice on the phone earlier in the day as she commuted to work. These moments served as anchors, pulling me back to the present.

A welcome shift in my mood accompanied the sound of the doorbell. Instantly, my thoughts pivoted to the imminent meeting that held the promise of redirecting my focus and infusing purpose into the monotony of my days. Opening the door, I was greeted by his friendly demeanour, his cheerful voice breaking through the silence, 'Hello. It's so wonderful to finally meet you.'

'Come in,' I replied with genuine excitement, mustering a brave smile. Desperate for change, I pushed aside any thoughts that trying to take on a job in my current state was not only impractical, it was lunacy. I would find a way to manage. There seemed no choice.

The rapport between us was instant as I openly shared my past work experiences. As we began compiling a list of industries where my skills could be applied, I was astonished at the array of opportunities he envisioned. My apprehension mounted as the conversation shifted towards potential retraining and manageable job prospects. Consciously, I ignored the nagging doubts hinting at the unfeasibility of employment. In my quest to discover something to fill my days and occupy my mind, I momentarily brushed aside the overwhelming magnitude of my current situation with a blind determination.

The inability to work and give back, constantly stirred feelings of unworthiness. *Who was I if I couldn't give in some capacity?* It was a delicate dance between hope and the harsh reality of my condition.

In the latter half of our meeting, the counsellor detailed my skills and attributes he had identified that would assist in writing a new resume. As we worked on my professional profile, enumerating my skills and strengths, I felt the familiar embarrassment of articulating positive words to characterise myself. This exercise was uncharted territory for me. I had never incorporated such self-praise into a resume. Shifting uneasily in my chair, a thought lingered, *Wouldn't an employer view this as boastful?*

Feeling the discomfort intensify, I couldn't shake the question, *Wasn't it humbler to let others notice your strengths?* In a soft, self-aware laugh, I admitted, 'I don't enjoy writing these things about myself.'

'Why not?' he asked.

'It doesn't feel comfortable,' I replied.

'But it's true. This *is* you,' he reassured, walking me through the verifiable truths of my profile. Despite the evidence, I found the words both confronting and difficult to acknowledge. The notion of speaking positively about myself clashed with the echoes of a childhood belief that resounded in my ears, 'Self-praise is no praise.' The very idea of acknowledging and vocalising my positive traits felt like an act of boasting.

Setting the resume aside for later completion, we shifted our focus to the list of potential options for retraining and future employment. Among the possibilities discussed, opportunities with the Cora Barclay Centre, the school for deaf and hearing-impaired children, stood out. This resonated as the most promising option and I knew that employment there was contingent on additional training. Deep down, I understood that my current health didn't permit immediate employment, but this process was a meaningful stepping stone, laying the groundwork for the day when I would be well enough to return to work.

With the support of the career advisor and guidance from the Cora Barclay Centre, I eagerly enrolled in the training program that would pave the way for me to work with hearing-impaired children as my health improved. I felt like a child anticipating their first ride at an amusement park. Excitedly sitting to begin the first online module, I embraced this opportunity for both a daily distraction and a new avenue of learning. Finally, I would have something meaningful to focus on and talk about.

The material proved to be both novel and engaging, and I felt a positive shift in my mental state, sensing I was progressing toward a purposeful goal. The idea of working with children in a field that promised both benefit and reward lifted my spirits. I eagerly anticipated my daily study sessions to absorb the knowledge required for the job.

However, my initial enthusiasm was soon met with the emergence of significant challenges stemming from my memory issues. I struggled to retain information from each lesson. It became evident I needed substantial repetition, echoing my experience from the photography course. Lessons were revisited three to four times over. A troubling thought surfaced, *Perhaps it wasn't only the complexity of photography; maybe there's something more going on?*

Reflecting on the daily challenges of misplacing items, forgetting tasks and general organisation challenges, I decided, *I'll need to work harder.* The journey ahead appeared demanding, yet the underlying determination to overcome these obstacles and pursue my goal remained unwavering.

I pressed on, fuelled by the deep desire to find a way to work and reshape my life. However, staring at the screen and reading intensified my eye and head pain. Fatigue and brain fog also increased their grip, but I remained steadfast, refusing to let these challenges hinder my progress. Battling through, I pushed aside the nagging sense I might be causing more harm to myself each day.

At the end of each section, tests awaited. Attempting to comprehend them felt like deciphering a foreign language. As I stared blankly at the questions on the screen, I felt a surge of panic. *Where was the information?* Leaning my head into my hands, my mind went blank. I closed my eyes and tried to focus, repeating to myself, 'Come on, you've learnt this. You know this.' Squirming in my chair, re-reading the questions, I thought, *I must have lost concentration in that section.* Going back to my notes, I revisited the topic. Yet, it was as if I had never encountered the information before.

Returning to the test, my heart raced as I attempted to complete the answers and move on to the next question. Once again, my mind was blank, and my heart sank. Repetition was helping me grasp the content at the time, but retention proved elusive. The struggle against cognitive hurdles persisted, a constant reminder of the intricate challenges woven into my pursuit of personal and professional growth.

Throughout my studies, the toll on my wellbeing became increasingly apparent. Fatigue weighed me down, pain surged and my self-esteem plummeted as my memory issues came to the forefront. The futility of my efforts loomed large, and thoughts of giving up cast a shadow over my progress. I felt an overwhelming sense of failure. If I struggled to learn something new, how could I navigate the challenges of a future job? 'What's the point of this life!' I cried out in despair in my empty home.

With pain unabated and the simplest aspects of daily life slipping further from my grasp, I turned to my GP, desperately seeking additional solutions. All hope of positive change in my life seemed lost. Trying to find purpose seemed futile and my pain was at an all-time high. As we delved into the discussion about work, she gently proposed, 'Rather than looking at roles with significant responsibilities, maybe you can consider a simple volunteer role down the track. Currently, you still need to focus on managing your pain and daily living.' Glancing in her direction, I noticed the emotion on her face as she delivered words challenging for me to hear. The thought crossed my mind, *She must think I'm delusional.* Shame took hold. I looked away, confronted by words I knew were true but couldn't bring myself to acknowledge. Trapped like a caged animal, suffocated by the limitations of my situation, every fibre in my being rebelled against my harsh reality. The significant impairment of my abilities, while recognised on some level, clashed with my desperate desire to cling to hope, to believe this situation wasn't permanent. It felt like a battle for my life, and the expectations of others added to the weight. With a twinge of embarrassment, I tried to redeem myself with a tearful nod, a silent acknowledgment of the painful truth. I hadn't been able to find a suitable option for returning to work because there wasn't one.

The weight of loss was tangible. My body ached with sorrow. I had to once again accept employment was off the table for now. Many in the online support group detailed their inability to work due to their pain, but I didn't want the same outcome.

Redirecting my focus, I conceded pain relief strategies had to continue to take precedence. If I could gain control over that, perhaps it would pave the way for a return to retraining or exploring work options in the future. My life had taken yet another turn, and while acceptance was a bitter pill, I had to believe it somehow held the promise of a different path towards healing and renewed possibilities.

I exited my GP's office once again, referral in hand for a new pain physician who specialised in facial pain. As I called to book the appointment, I wondered how much longer I could endure the constant ebb and flow of shattered hopes and dreams.

17.

NO STONE LEFT UNTURNED

*'Hoping for the best, preparing for the worst,
and unsurprised for anything in between.'*
Maya Angelou

Stepping into the pain clinic, housed in a magnificent old building surrounded by sprawling gardens, I couldn't discern whether my nerves stemmed from excitement or fear. Ascending the stairs to the consultation rooms, my legs felt heavy, burdened by the weight of anticipation. Self-doubt crept in, and I began questioning myself, *Am I wasting my time persisting in my search for answers?* Uncertainty clouded my thoughts. *Would the physician grasp the severity of my pain and the struggle of living with it? Was there any purpose in coming here?* A nagging fearful thought lingered, *Would he confirm that it is permanent and nothing could be done?* The repetition of hearing my case was the worst many of my specialists had encountered led me to believe perhaps they were subtly conveying, 'There's no hope. You simply have to live with it.' *Couldn't anyone see it's not possible to live with it forever?* As I settled into the waiting room, I silently hoped the physician would at least be kind.

Understandably, after enduring 18 months of debilitating pain, my tolerance was wearing thin and my stamina was dwindling. The weariness from seeking help from various therapists and professionals had taken its toll. However, the enduring nature of the torment coupled with my desire for some normalcy in life continued to fuel a desperate search for relief. Pushing aside any lingering doubt, I rested my head back in the chair, closed my eyes and quietly repeated my mantra: 'I will not let you beat me.'

As the pain physician walked out to greet me, his cheerful smile immediately lifted my mood, making me feel at ease. Stepping into his consultation room, I was struck by its size and elegance – a space that felt warm, inviting and notably lacking the clinical atmosphere of many medical rooms. Reminding myself of his reputation for expertise in the field of face pain research, I set aside any doubts. *There had to be alternative solutions to alleviate my symptoms,* I thought. *Please let him be the person who can help me.*

My eyes filled with tears as he immediately validated my pain experience with words full of compassion and understanding. 'I've read all your notes and can see you've had a dreadful time of things. It really is a cruel pain and people find it difficult to understand because it's largely invisible. I mean, you look so well.' Instantly, tears of relief silently fell. I quickly reached a hand to my tears, wiping them away before they landed on my cheek. Nodding at the acknowledgement, I closed my eyes and exhaled with relief. *He understood.*

My thoughts immediately flashed back to a recent conversation with a friend. She had witnessed me enduring some difficult moments and challenged me on hiding so much from others. 'I think you need to let people see you like this so that they can understand,' she said.

'But I can't just curl up in the foetal position and fall apart,' I replied, guilt-ridden just thinking about the distress it would cause others.

'Sometimes I think you should. Maybe then people will realise what you're going through.' she replied, her voice full of concern.

At times I did want to pick up the phone to call a friend and say, 'I don't know what to do, I'm struggling.' But there was no solution. *What could they do?*

As my thoughts returned to the consultation room, I replied, 'Yes, I work hard on my health and try to do all I can but you're right, no-one can see what it's really like. I try to put on a brave face.' I was grateful for his validating words of acknowledgement.

During an open discussion about my experience to date and the treatments I'd tried, his sense of humour had me stifling laughter to avoid further pain. As he listened and shared his views, his positive energy and enthusiasm, coupled with his compassion, had an uplifting effect on me. He explained why cold weather exacerbated my nerve pain and supported my strategy to head for warmer climates during the Adelaide winter. Following our discussion, he proceeded with a physical assessment of my face. 'I'm sorry I have to cause you pain while I do this,' he said, his face filled with genuine concern.

'It's okay. I'm used to it,' I replied. His effervescent nature and positivity filled me with confidence and while I dreaded his touch, I understood he needed to assess the damage. Watching my face, he gently dragged the tightly rolled corner of a tissue over different areas. 'Can you feel that?' he asked as he looked for signs of any sensory loss or extreme sensitivity to touch. Flinching as the tissue touched my skin, it felt like I'd encountered an electric fence, not a tissue. Tensing, I tried to sit still and not pull away at each touch. My eyes were wide with fear as my face spasmed throughout the assessment. The light touch of the tissue initiated the sensation of ants crawling over my face in some areas, piercing pain in others, yet, in other areas, little to no sensation at all. 'Sorry,' he said as my cheek twitched, sending sharp pain shooting through my eye. 'That's enough. It's very clear this is quite severe.'

Shaking his head, he sat in front of me and went on to explain my nerve pain using the analogy of an electric guitar, likening it to the piercing sound of feedback when the amplifier is turned up too loud. Just a light touch on the strings can cause the amplifier to give a screeching sound. As he connected this to my pain experience, I understood then that the damage to my nerves meant the nerves didn't send messages from the skin to the brain in the same way they once did. Instead, they were now sending confused amplified messages. Nodding slowly as his explanation sunk in, the permanent nature of the nerve damage was becoming clearer. 'I've never had it explained that way,' I replied. 'It makes sense. So, if the nerves are damaged permanently, does it mean this pain will never go away?'

Sharing the confronting reality with me, he explained, 'The head is the most sensitive to pain. There is no distance between the stimulus of the nerve pain and the message getting to the brain. It's instantaneous. There's no escaping it and this is a severe case. The most important thing we have to do with you is ensure there is little stress in your life.' As I nodded, he added, 'It's unlikely you will ever be completely free from the pain given its severity and prolonged duration but there are some other options we can explore.'

Clinging to every word he spoke, I listened for evidence there was hope something would eventually work. Shifting nervously in my chair, I enquired, 'What else is there to try if all the other medications failed?' My eyes pooled with tears as I added, 'The side effects from the drugs left me struggling to function. I can't go back to that state again.'

'There are other medications with different mechanisms of action we haven't tried yet and we can also try lignocaine patches. Have you tried a TENS machine for pain relief?'

'A TENS machine? I can't imagine what electrical impulses delivered to my face would feel like,' I replied, my face full of fear. After explaining various medications, we settled on applying lignocaine, a local anaesthetic, to my face for 12 hours each night to try and numb the nerve.

The lignocaine patches proved excruciating. The wet, cold patches were intolerable to apply and given my most intense pain was around my eye and inside my ear, it proved difficult to find an effective way to use them. Over the next few months, we explored numerous approaches. Our exploration extended to various medications, including multiple opioids, yet none proved effective. In a seemingly unconventional approach, we even experimented with connecting a TENS machine to my face. Together, we left no stone unturned, trying every possible avenue in the pursuit of relief. Unfortunately, the medications didn't seem to alter the pain, only my alertness. The side effects had a profound impact on my ability to function. They proved significantly challenging for daily living. While I persisted, my inability to tolerate the adverse effects meant he had to proceed cautiously with what was prescribed.

After many unsuccessful attempts to find relief, I returned to the clinic late in 2017. Wearing disappointment on his face as we discussed the limited options left, he said, 'I'd like you to see a colleague of mine, a specialist pain management neurosurgeon, to see if there's any surgical procedure for the trigeminal nerve which might be helpful.' While I thought brain surgery was extreme, I had researched this option in desperation. I was prepared to undertake brain surgery if it would stop the pain. Whatever it took.

Leaving the clinic with a renewed sense of hope that surgery might offer a solution, he placed his hand on my arm and reassured me he would continue to assist me. 'I don't want to be that person who says I can't do any more for you.' His thoughtful gesture left me confident he was committed to continuing the search for solutions. Throughout our interactions, his compassion and understanding of the severity of my pain and the challenges of living with it provided great comfort. His support and understanding was a great source of strength.

Imagine if I could have surgery and return to my old life. Everyone would be relieved to have the 'old' me back, I thought, sitting in the car. The invisible nature of my pain continued to pose challenges and it was easy to see how others could assume my situation was better than it was. I was nervously planning a trip overseas to celebrate a combined 50th birthday celebration with some lovely friends the following year and was desperate to find some relief by then. Maybe surgery would be the answer. It was one thing to spend most days alone managing my condition, but it would require a mammoth effort to do so in public every day.

18.

ALL HOPE IS GONE

> *'Do not resist your pain. Surrender to the grief, despair, fear, loneliness or what form the suffering takes. Witness it without labelling it mentally. Allow it to be there. Embrace it. Then see how the miracle of surrender transmutes deep suffering into deep peace.'*
> Eckhart Tolle

Two weeks later, I walked into the neurosurgeons' room with a hopeful heart. An intense mix of emotions consumed me as I sat in the waiting room. Leafing through one of the coffee table books, it opened to the relatable words, *'Pain can sweep away everything but your day-to-day survival.'*[8] My fingers nervously tapped my legs in anticipation. I was placing all my hope in this neurosurgeon. While the prospect of brain surgery seemed drastic, I knew I was prepared to go to any length to resolve the pain. My body tensed, recognising this was the finale, the last resort. If surgery couldn't provide relief, then all hope would be lost. *Am I really here on my own contemplating brain surgery?* The thought swirled in my mind, and I shook my head in disbelief. *Why do these appointments fall when John is away?* Tearfully, I pushed the sadness aside. *The less he heard, the better,* I resolved. While John often couldn't find the words to express his pain, I knew the sadness and helplessness he felt was no different to mine. We loved each other deeply and felt each other's pain like it was our own.

Raising my gaze as the neurosurgeon called my name, I set the book aside and followed him into the consultation room, my legs unsteady. Armed with a list of numerous unanswered questions, I hesitated, unsure now if I truly wanted the answers. Choking back tears, I attempted to provide an accurate description of my pain. He meticulously undertook his assessment, testing for areas of altered sensation as he moved about my face. Once again, the conclusive response was definitive – there existed significant nerve damage in multiple areas of my face.

'What guaranteed surgical options are there?' I asked, bracing myself for the answer after he shared his assessment.

Unprepared for the simplicity of his response, he uttered, 'None.'

My stomach lurched. 'None?' I echoed in a whisper, seeking clarification.

The neurosurgeon elaborated, 'There are some neurosurgical options for neuropathic facial pain, however the outcomes for PHTN have never been particularly good historically or in my own experience.' He proceeded to explain the intricacies of PHTN, emphasising its association with irreparable damage to both the peripheral and central nervous systems.

Gently, he walked me through the four surgical options: peripheral nerve stimulation, requiring the insertion of electrodes under the skin on my face; motor cortex stimulation, more invasive, requiring electrodes placed on the surface of the brain to control pain signals; deep brain stimulation, more invasive again as it implants a device deep inside the brain, and finally, dorsal root entry zone (DREZ), lesioning of the brain stem to interrupt the pain signal. Feeling my hands shake, my heart raced with the rush of adrenaline from the thought that one of these could stop my pain. Despite the absence of guaranteed surgical options, I was willing to take any necessary risk in the pursuit of finding relief.

'What option would be most effective?' I asked.

His next words echoed the reality I had dreaded. Little to no hope accompanied any of the neurosurgical options. Most had not been employed to treat my condition at all. Understanding the trial of TENS had been unhelpful and had exacerbated my pain, he indicated that even the least invasive, peripheral nerve stimulation, would be unlikely to offer relief. Later it would be confirmed by the oral and maxillofacial surgeon that while these operations can be successful for idiopathic trigeminal neuralgia, for viral induced trigeminal neuralgia, the changes are deep within the brain beyond where surgery can reach.

'Can we cut the nerve?' I ventured.

'That's old and very risky. It's a destructive procedure and could leave you worse off,' he cautioned.

As hope gradually drained away, I posed the question always lingering in my mind, the question no-one had yet been able to provide a hopeful response to: 'I've had no improvement in almost two years. Is there still a chance I will recover?'

'The biggest predictor of recovery is the time you've had it. Age and immunity also come into it. There is more chance of recovery the younger you are,' he replied.

Tears welled up in my eyes, and my lips trembled with the weight of my situation. Reality was sinking in, and my limbs suddenly felt weak, almost numb. 'But how do I live with it?' I asked, my voice barely audible.

Slowly raising his shoulders, he replied, compassion evident in his voice, 'It's difficult.' Time seemed to stand still, and the room felt like it was spinning. Breaking the heavy silence, he explained the long-term challenge. 'It's like a cherry picker. Pluck the best out of a cookie jar: mindfulness, pain psychology, hypnosis, whatever brings some relief. It's not an all-or-nothing, but if you get a few percent relief from each, it all adds up.'

Nodding, I felt all hope fading, yet I bravely maintained my composure. I was already doing those things and had even tried hypnosis for a period. There was no magic bullet. No miracle cure. The futility of my situation was suddenly real. Even the pursuit of suitable pain relief could no longer bring purpose to my days.

As I stood up to go, I enquired about the trial of a Ketamine infusion suggested to me at the pain clinic. He agreed it could be worth considering, as they had seen temporary relief in a patient with a different nerve pain condition. Thanking him for his time, I walked out the door, holding back tears I feared would never stop if I let them out.

Leaving yet another medical facility with little hope of change to my situation, I contained my emotions until I opened my car door. Falling onto the seat, I lay my head back and let warm tears flow. Sobbing, my body shook all over as I released the bitter anguish of my continued failed attempts to find relief. Tears I had held back for almost two years, hidden behind hope, could no longer be contained. Overwhelmed with the emptiness of being alone in my grief, I called a friend who was waiting to hear the outcome. Hardly able to speak, a sob escaped from a place so deep I didn't know it existed. 'There's no hope. It's finished. I can't keep hearing this anymore,' I sobbed through the agony of words I uttered but had hoped never to speak.

Hearing the anguish in my friend's voice, her consoling words of deep understanding, comprehending what this meant for me, I crumbled. Feeling as if I had left my body, a dark shadow suddenly filled every space within me, accompanied by an indescribable emptiness. I knew I had lost the battle. Every part of my being felt hollow. The silence that filled the air as she listened attentively to my sobs, holding space for me to openly express the gut-wrenching pain, marked the moment I finally let down my defences. No longer able to bear the intense loneliness behind my protective mask, I unleashed all the emotions I had hidden from myself and others.

Her gentle and empathetic response, her skill in simply being present, enabled me to feel acknowledged even in the absence of words. She provided a cocoon of safety where I could authentically express myself. Not everyone possesses the capacity to sit with another's pain and create room for catharsis and I was acutely aware of the feelings of helplessness it evoked in others. While I knew my friend might carry the weight of this, I also understood my vulnerability was secure with her and, to some extent, I knew she could navigate it.

Returning home, I walked inside, my legs weakened with exhaustion. Weary and unable to summon enough energy to prepare food, I reached for a tube of eye drops and curled up on the couch. Propping myself up on the cushions to alleviate the familiar dizziness, I applied drops to my eye, seeking respite from the grating discomfort. *Relief.* Exhaling a sigh, I allowed myself to close my eyes.

Although I was once again home alone wishing John was with me, I had never felt so grateful to have a friend to share yet another loss with. Her words as we had ended the call filled a void of loneliness in that moment, a void that seemed ever-present, 'This is big, Denise. It really is. I'll always be here for you, you know that.' The nagging fear of overloading my friend surfaced. Gently shaking my head, one thought alone remained, *This is too much for anyone.*

As I lay on the couch, my nerves sending searing jolts in every direction across my face, I felt the familiar clench in my stomach. I feared what lay ahead for me. Many years later, I would learn not only of the anguish my friend had felt during and after that phone call, but also of the relief she experienced. Through my emotional release, she heard acceptance – that I had to abandon the fight to find solutions.

19.

THE BOTTOM OF THE BARREL

'Acceptance doesn't mean resignation; it means understanding that something is what it is and that there's got to be a way through it.'
Michael J Fox

I drifted through the following days in a fog. Numb from the harsh truth of having to navigate life with no prospects of relief, I adopted a new routine of morning walks from our home to the ocean. The weather had warmed, and the spring winds had subsided enough to allow me to venture outdoors without the looming threat of an afternoon with my head in a bucket. I felt constantly torn, weighing the benefits of a walk outdoors against the potential consequences.

Despite the risks of aggravating my symptoms, I sought solace in nature. The Torrens River, flowing behind our home and leading all the way to the ocean, offered a sanctuary accessible through our back gate. Stepping outside one morning, in the week following my appointment with the neurosurgeon, I winced as the air itself felt like a torment. My breath shortened as the tendrils of nerve pain made their usual entrance, crawling across my face like an irritating spider. The familiar stabbing sensation deep in my ear soon followed.

In those moments, I sought refuge in a technique learnt from the pain psychologist: focus on three things you can see, two things you can hear, and one thing you can smell. As I walked along the path, frantically scanning my surroundings for distractions, I remained oblivious to passersby. Regardless of my discomfort, there was a semblance of normalcy in being outdoors. Being in the warmth of the sun became a welcome change for a body that now seemed no longer capable of warming itself. Watching a family feed carrots to horses ahead, I smiled, only to wince and push my finger into my ear as that simple facial expression aggravated the nerves. Tears welled up, but I pressed on, returning to my distraction strategy. If nothing else, I would become intimately familiar with every sight and sound along that river as the months unfolded.

Reaching the hill provided a beautiful view of the sea. I paused and absorbed the scenery. Despite the assault to my nerves from the outdoor breeze, I was glad I had made the effort. *Will I ever be able to walk outdoors pain-free?* I pondered. With the prospect of one last chance at pain medication around the corner, I had decided the suggested trial of Ketamine would mark my final endeavour to seek relief through drugs. I was exhausted from trying every possible solution, only to face repeated failure each time I allowed myself to hope 'this next one' would work. With disappointment after disappointment, my resolve to keep trying was rapidly diminishing. I'd grown weary of the distress it caused yet another practitioner, observing the pity and helplessness in their expressions while they tried everything to assist me. Ketamine seemed like an extreme measure, but I had nothing left to lose. Turning around to make my way back home, I put all thoughts of 'what if' aside.

Returning to the pain clinic the following day, the physician discussed the outcome of the neurologist's assessment with me. 'I had hoped there was a possibility of something new out there we didn't know about,' he said. 'I think we give the Ketamine a try and see if that can make a difference. I'll do some investigations and find someone who can make a sublingual version of it, a troche that sits under your tongue, so you can trial it at home.'

Within two weeks, I received the news a compounding pharmacist had been able to make the Ketamine in sublingual form, and it was ready for me to collect. Having now researched information about the drug, I was humoured by the fact I was off to collect what I had discovered was a sought-after street drug termed, 'Special K'. On the way to the pharmacy, John and I chuckled at the fact we were going to collect Ketamine. However, I held complete faith in the pain physician and neurosurgeon.

When I arrived to pick up my prescription, a pharmacist was summoned to speak to me. After ushering us into a small consultation room, she explained I would need to be under 24/7 supervision throughout the 10-day trial. John and I exchanged frowns, our eyes widening in surprise. 'My husband works away in the mine. He's only home for six days.'

'Well, it must be administered under supervision because I expect you will experience side effects.' Frowning, I looked at her apprehensively and asked, 'What have other people experienced when they used Ketamine in this way?'

'It's the first time we've made it like this.' Raising my eyebrows, I shrugged my shoulders, smiling inwardly. 'Oh well, it's worth a try.'

Early in January 2018, we made plans for when I would begin the trial. During the week John was away at work, I called to check on his father as his health had rapidly declined. After speaking with his brother, it was evident things were dire. I immediately made the decision to book John a flight to see his father the day he was to fly home from the mine. On his arrival in Adelaide, I explained the plans and he replied, 'I can't do that. You have to do the Ketamine trial.'

'Don't worry about me, I'll sort that out. You need to go and see your father.' Conflicted, he challenged the plans, but I reminded him this was more important right now. Trying to consider the needs of everyone, I could see his conflict. 'I'll be okay. Just go,' I said.

As I drove him back to the airport, I realised I lacked a plan. My pain had become so challenging to control I was desperate to commence the trial simply for relief. Seeking assistance at any time was uncomfortable but requesting someone to be by my side for the trial brought immense unease. Uncertain of what lay ahead, I wasn't sure about the potential outcomes. The pain physician had reiterated that while Ketamine is an old licensed drug used as a general anaesthetic, sublingual Ketamine for the management of neuropathic pain is an off-label use. He also mentioned the pharmacy had noted the typical side effects at higher doses included dizziness, a 'spaced-out' feeling and hallucinations. However, I was to start on a very low dose and gradually increase it.

On the Saturday morning, two days after John departed, I approached my daughter as she came downstairs. 'Will you be around home today?' It was asking a lot of her.

'I'll be in and out a bit. Why?' she responded.

'Well, I need to start this trial and I wondered if you could be around when I take the first dose. I have to take it every six hours for 10 days but I'm not sure what it will be like once it starts working.' Indicating she would be available for the next two hours, I decided to start. John would return the following night, so I wouldn't be long managing it on my own, and a friend had offered to be with me if needed once John went back to work.

Within a minute of placing the troche under my tongue to dissolve, the room started spinning, and my eyes struggled to stay open. Moving quickly to the lounge, I collapsed into the recliner, sedated within minutes. Waking over two hours later, I began vomiting. At the six-hour mark, only partially aware of my surroundings, my daughter assisted me to the bathroom before I took the next dose. The same reaction occurred. That night, I said to her, 'I should be okay on my own tonight because I'll only take it once I'm in bed ready for sleep.' Uncomfortable with what she'd witnessed, and unbeknown to me, she changed her plans and stayed. While my memory of that night is hazy, she recalls coming in to check on me, hearing me vomiting through the night.

By the following afternoon, my daughter proactively reached out to the physician on his mobile, a generous provision he had offered to enable us to stay connected throughout the trial so he could monitor my progress. Advising her to reduce my dose by half, we pushed on. *I wish she did not have to witness this.* Facing

THE BOTTOM OF THE BARREL

a similar reaction, we contacted him again the next day. 'We are fast approaching barrel bottom,' he noted. 'It's like it's overdosing you, but it shouldn't be at that dose. Try a quarter dose and let me know how that goes.' Although it reduced sedation time, the side effects persisted.

In the midst of this period, a close friend vividly recalls calling me while I attempted to shower. 'You were just so frightened,' she recalls sadly. 'I remember thinking, enough. This is enough. No more. It was so hard and so painful to see you try so many things and come to yet another brick wall.'

Over the next two days, I tried to persist with the trial but the cranial pressure intensified, escalating the pain, and hindering sleep. Almost one week into the trial, I was in terrible pain and feeling so disillusioned I abandoned it. There were no tears, just overwhelming emptiness. The last resort, gone. Enough setbacks. No more.

Western medicine had explored every avenue it could, and I found myself standing alone. It was me, my head, and I. I had reached the point of being done with medications, done with assessments. I was done with a life dominated by medical appointments. I was done with a never-ending cycle of trial and error. I was done with pushing myself to make it to appointments every day simply to fight for my life, a life that seemed to lack any purpose beyond survival. With no sign of relief on the horizon, my only option was to turn further inward and concentrate on planning a life around the pain, no matter how restricted that life might be. I believed I had hit rock bottom. I didn't know yet there was further to fall – again and again.

20.

A LIFELINE

'Maybe the journey isn't so much about becoming anything. Maybe it's about un-becoming everything that isn't really you, so you can be who you were meant to be in the first place.'
Paul Coelho

After the trial, my situation felt more hopeless than ever. I was depleted on every level. Despite the pain physician's optimism about potential new medications, my mind glazed over at the thought. I felt almost relieved when I was invited to participate in a new nerve pain medication study but wasn't available for the trial period. The pursuit of pain relief, once my sole focus, now felt like a closed chapter. After my failed attempt at finding relief through Ketamine, a sense of resignation settled into my bones. The tireless quest for relief had provided a temporary purpose, a flicker of hope. But now it was over, I was left confronted with new questions of purpose. *What remained for me? How could I craft a life that felt worth living alongside the pain?*

Two weeks after the trial in January 2018, my daughter left home for the country to begin her career. I missed her presence, particularly in John's absences, however I felt relieved she was somewhat protected during this difficult phase. She had witnessed enough. Almost two years had passed on this journey, yet grief and loss still weighed heavily on me. With no relief in sight, the hopelessness of the situation felt even more profound, amplifying an unparalleled sense of isolation. I felt devoid of life. I had lost my sense of self, stripped of everything that once defined me. The persistent question, *Who am I now?* pervaded my thoughts.

One evening early in April, after John returned home from the mine, we settled on the couch and exchanged stories about our week. I confided in John about feeling lost, unsure of how to navigate life without relief.

'We have our holiday to Europe in a few months which will be fantastic,' John reassured me. 'It'll be great for you to have a break from everything and spend time with friends.'

'I just hope I can manage okay,' I replied, my apprehension evident. 'I have no idea how it'll work, but at least the warm weather will help.'

Despite my excitement for the trip, I couldn't shake my concerns about how I would be perceived if I had difficulty managing my pain. I had communicated I didn't want my health issues to impact anyone and that I would find ways to manage myself, but it didn't stop me feeling anxious about letting down our friends during the holiday. We had carefully planned the trip to make it as manageable as possible. I would have my camera with me all the time, knowing photography served as a valuable distraction from the pain. I had arranged to arrive earlier than John and would be staying with friends in Germany. This would allow ample time to rest and adjust to the time zone while escaping the cold Adelaide winter.

While I was nervous about managing an overseas holiday, a cruise seemed the perfect choice for my condition. I found comfort in knowing I could retreat and rest if needed.

Walking into the study to check my emails the following morning, I stared at the screen of my laptop, once primarily a work tool. As I waited for it to start up, I leant back in my chair and gently closed my eyes, reflecting on my challenges.

Feeling like a caged animal, I remained desperate to find a way to change my reality, yet I struggled to keep pace with even the most basic demands of daily life, like showering and washing my hair, or preparing food and paying bills. I questioned my value. *Did I still have anything meaningful to contribute? Did I even matter anymore?* Even with depleted energy reserves, I still persisted in attempting to be present for others, as the fear of losing connections still hung in the air like a damp mist. Hypersensitive to any hint of judgement through words or actions, my confidence in relationships had continued to wane. It was a delicate balance, being caught between the fear of rejection and the longing for acceptance. I dared to hope for understanding and solidarity.

A simple expression of empathy, a heartfelt acknowledgment of the relentless nature of my situation, or a warm embrace, were like rays of sunshine in my darkest moments. Even the simplest words carried immense weight and propelled me forward. However, those moments of feeling misunderstood, dismissed or judged, still echoed louder.

As time passed, I had gradually become more attuned to the differences in how individuals responded throughout some of my more difficult times. To adapt, I became chameleon-like, gauging when to open up and when to remain guarded. When to wear the mask and when not to. Navigating social interactions still felt like tiptoeing through a minefield, never sure of the right words to say or the appropriate time to speak up.

Despite experiencing shingles twice since my initial bout, stark reminders of my body's limitations, I still pushed myself beyond my capabilities. I neglected crucial pacing strategies essential for managing my energy and pain. Not listening to my body, giving more than I had, would eventually lead to four further bouts of shingles over the next five years.

There were many moments I wanted to step over the cliff edge I teetered on and allow myself to fall apart, to scream, to give up life like some in the support group had done. Their final attempt at relief. During these times, I retreated, often leaving phone calls unanswered to hide my despair and spare any awkwardness until I gathered strength. *If I answered, what could I talk about anyway?* At times I responded to questions with a question so I could avoid sharing. While it eliminated awkward silences, it fuelled feelings of aloneness. Some saw through this and persisted with their unanswered questions. For this, I was grateful.

Occasionally, I allowed myself brief moments to silently weep in private, despite the impact on my face and the accompanying guilt of giving in to my emotions. *'I need to be stronger than this,'* I whispered, my eyes now focused back on the computer screen as my mind returned to the present.

Opening my email program, I was greeted by a daunting sight: over 500 unread emails. Administrative tasks, once simple, had become overwhelming. As I scrolled through the emails, scanning for urgent matters, one message stood out among the rest. It was from Heidi, the life coach and founder of the Queensland health retreat I had attended back in 2016. She was reaching out to past participants, offering them a chance to join a 12-week beta program called Life School.

Life School. I certainly feel like I need an education in how to live this life. I chuckled to myself. The description explained the program aimed to create balance in participants' lives, a concept which felt elusive amidst managing life with chronic pain. *Balance?* I thought. *My focus on health has taken over my life. There was no balance.*

The program aimed to help participants visualise their desired reality and overcome any inner obstacles preventing them from achieving it. Despite my scepticism and the little energy I had, the timing was ironic and the program seemed like a lifeline.

What immediately resonated with me though, were Heidi's words highlighting how easily we can lose touch with ourselves in the face of harsh wake-up calls. There was no denying the magnitude of the situation I was confronted with, nor that I was lost. *Did I have the capacity to engage in the program, though?*

Tears welled in my eyes as I allowed myself to imagine a different life, a change of course. The monotony and solitude of my days, dominated by medical appointments and the incessant struggle against pain, continued to feel like a slow erosion of my soul.

A LIFELINE

Determined to improve my quality of life, I resolved to embrace this opportunity for change. I had nothing to lose. The program offered hope. Responding promptly to her email, I exhaled a sigh of relief and typed, 'I would love to take part.' *Please, let this be the guidance I need to find a solution for living with my condition,* I silently hoped as I clicked send.

21.

LIFE SCHOOL

'She never seemed shattered; to me, she was a breathtaking mosaic of the battles she's won.'
Matt Baker

As I walked along the riverbank behind our home the following week, I couldn't shake the anticipation building. The start of the personal growth program was just around the corner and it had me reflecting on the path I had travelled since my time at the health retreat. Despite regular pain psychology, implementing meditation and yoga, and my diet undergoing a radical transformation, a sense of direction still eluded me. My focus seemed solely fixated on survival, on merely pushing through each passing hour. The mental effort it demanded left me exhausted, constantly battling to manage my mindset.

The cool air on the walk proved too much for me, and after only 20 minutes, I returned home. Resting on the couch with my heated wheat bag, doubts began to creep in as I contemplated the upcoming program. *Would it offer enough to help me make changes? Was change even possible? Would Heidi view my struggles with pity but have no answers? Would she simply suggest I accept my circumstances as they are?* Accepting my condition was one thing, but accepting this life was another. I couldn't, and I didn't want this for my friends and family. Signing up for the program was undoubtably a decision fraught with uncertainty.

Despite my apprehensions, I viewed the program as a gift, a rare opportunity to receive intensive guidance in creating a more desirable life. Heidi's extraordinary reputation for bringing about change meant it would be like having a golden ticket to personal growth. With nothing to lose, I wanted to prove to myself I had given my all. Feeling myself slipping, I knew I needed help taking action. I couldn't see a way through on my own. My tank was beyond empty.

Clicking on the Zoom link on the first day of the program, I waited nervously for Heidi's face to appear on the screen. *Well, here goes,* I thought, as I glanced at the open notebook on my study desk. *Time to dig deeper.* Suddenly, her cheerful face appeared. 'Hello everyone,' she said, her enthusiastic energy immediately drawing me in.

From day one, there was no option but to embrace vulnerability. With three Zoom sessions scheduled each week and significant work in-between implementing all we learnt, the program proved to be intense. I embraced all on offer from the outset. Each week the eight of us participating were expected to upload videos, sharing our reflections and progress. Heidi saw through each of us, every pattern, belief and behaviour, challenging everything we shared with expertise. With her wisdom and insight, she immediately gained our trust.

Like the health retreat two years prior, I was again confronted with all that was uncovered, but this time there was no escape. Accountability was deeply embedded in the program. Taking action was a non-negotiable. Heidi delved fearlessly into the depths of my thoughts, beliefs and fears. Almost instantly, she identified the extremity of my fear of withdrawing support from others to focus on myself.

As she expertly questioned me, it became immediately apparent that despite persistent signals from my body, I had a habit of continuing to neglect listening to it. 'Your identity is so tightly intertwined with providing for others, you're oblivious to the obstacle you've become to yourself,' she remarked. 'You've lost yourself in giving so much to others. Your job is to find yourself.' It was a harsh reality check.

All I could think was if only I could work again, I wouldn't have this issue. *Contributing is what I love to do. If I could do that, I'd be back to myself,* I thought. She guided me in recognising that, beyond teaching and being a mother and wife, I had lost sight of my purpose. When asked about my current purpose, I replied, 'To survive. Just to survive, that's all. But I want to find a way to live with this pain that makes living worthwhile. Statistically, so many succumb to this condition. I don't want to be one of them but it's getting harder and harder.'

As she challenged me to explore who I was, I felt reluctant to respond. I was the giver, the helper, the listener. In completing the task of redefining myself and who I wanted to be, my mind went blank. My life had undergone a profound change, and the exercise highlighted how ill-equipped I felt to navigate my condition when I was focused on prioritising the needs of others. Struggling to survive, I had no confidence in my ability to reinvent my life under seemingly insurmountable circumstances.

Both Heidi and the pain psychologist had highlighted my tendency to prioritise pleasing others at the expense of my own wellbeing. So, I was confronted with a consistent image of myself; in the process of my people pleasing behaviours, I had lost not only a sense of purpose but also my identity. Heidi pointed out, 'This is like self-punishment, giving so much. You need to focus on you, not on what everyone else wants you to be. Who do you want to be? It's time to focus on being, not doing.'

As I contemplated her suggestion, I began to grasp why I had lost my sense of purpose. My entire identity had revolved around serving others, being their support system, their rock in times of need. My career had also been centred on catering to the needs of others. With my capacity to help diminished, no wonder I felt lost.

Shifting uncomfortably in my chair, I recalled a recent moment when a close friend had handed me a book titled *People Pleasing*. With a playful chuckle, she remarked, 'Someone gave me this, but I think you need this more than I do.' Though I laughed along with her, inwardly I felt surprised at being seen as a people pleaser. *Was I? Or was I simply kind and thoughtful?* Despite a brief moment of internal questioning, I laughed at the gesture. I treasured the effortless simplicity of our warm, trusting friendship, her unwavering loyalty through every stage of my journey, and the calm, comforting presence she brought into my life. No offence was taken; instead, I wondered if she knew me better than I knew myself.

As the program unfolded, we delved deeper into an exploration of our beliefs, uncovering their origins. In the process, I confronted life experiences long suppressed, tucked away in corners too painful to revisit. These were experiences I did not think I was entitled to feel sad or angry about. The pervasive belief I should always strive to do better, to soldier on with life, continually resurfaced through the program, revealing how harshly I judged and pushed myself. I was prompted to take notice of the language I used in my self-talk, recognising its impact on my wellbeing and growth.

In a subsequent session, I was urged to pay attention to the source of my critical self-talk. Was it truly my own voice or was it the echo of someone else's, pushing me to strive for more, to do better, to work so hard at everything in pursuit of an elusive sense of worthiness? As I tuned in, a painful silence settled in me. I recognised the voices, distinct and familiar. In that moment of introspection, I softly acknowledged, 'No, it's not my voice, but I've come to believe it.'

Through her insightful questions, Heidi not only unearthed my fear of inadequacy but also exposed a deeply rooted fear of abandonment and rejection. Addressing the complexities of my situation, she stated, 'Your friends and family should be rallying around you now. It's time for you to accept help from others, not just be there for them.'

'I'm more accustomed to being the support for others, not so good at receiving or asking for it,' I admitted.

'Have you asked for help?' she inquired further.

Adjusting uncomfortably in my seat, I paused before responding, 'Honestly, I don't even know what would help. It's nice to have people around me to help ease the monotony but sometimes being around people exacerbates my pain and I end up feeling worse later. It depends how aware they are, but I'd rather endure the pain than be stuck on my own all the time. It's a tough balance.'

'What is your process for asking for help?' she probed. 'Some people don't know how to ask.'

'I emailed some information to close friends and family about my condition over a year ago. I didn't ask for much. It's not like it's fixable. I shared information about my condition and asked them to jolly me along and keep things normal. Company with a walk, a coffee, a visit. Since then, I've tried at times to be open about my situation if I'm asked, but not everyone understands or wants to know. Some don't engage or they avoid it so I try to be careful who I share with. Even though it's hard, I have to respect some don't want to know.'

'With what you're going through, people should be reaching out to you,' she commented.

'I'm lucky to have a handful of friends who do reach out. They keep showing up, and include me even when I'm not at my best. I don't have to say anything because they recognise what's going on and have no expectations on me.'

'Well stick with those people. But be clear in communicating with them what you need,' she suggested.

'I don't want to feel needy,' I confessed. 'Asking for company feels like an inconvenience. I feel guilty asking for help,' I added.

'You are feeling guilty for asking but also people don't always know you need help. People avoid discomfort like the plague. They probably don't know what to say. Sometimes we don't know what to do with a situation that can't be changed. Some people struggle with an uncomfortable situation.'

Her words struck a chord, resonating with the painful memories after losing my mother. During that time, some friends and family had been unsure what to say or do, avoiding me altogether. This felt like abandonment, leaving me to navigate my grief alone. The experience left me feeling incredibly isolated. These memories served as a poignant reminder of the complexities of human connection and the discomfort which often accompanies others' profound sorrow and uncertainty.

'Stop putting effort into the people who are not there. The feeling of being needy is coming from having to ask them for help. Everyone feels guilty asking for help, especially when you've been independent. It's how we often are. It should come from them, it should if they're good friends. Still have contact with them but cut off your energy.'

Stop putting energy in? If I didn't show up for others, would they still be there for me? I knew I was exerting too much energy trying to show up and my health was suffering, but stopping would require overriding my fear of being completely abandoned. Impossible.

'Because your face is so cheery no-one would know you're going through that much pain and discomfort. Every time I watch your videos I think, but you look so good. I also think part of the issue is you have always been the giver and support for them.'

As her words sank in, discomfort moved through my body like a dark shadow. In spite of my efforts to be a good friend, guilt, shame and a heavy sadness settled in at the reminder I could no longer offer the support I once did. My cognitive abilities now faltered, causing me to struggle through conversations. Listening drained me of energy as I tried to focus.

The simple acts of talking, smiling and laughing, once effortless, were now accompanied by pain and exhaustion. Even driving served as a painful reminder of my limitations. As the realisation set in that I was no longer the pillar of strength I once was, I felt embarrassed at being the one in need of help, the fallen one who could no longer stand tall. I also recognised the inherent difficulty in supporting someone facing a long-term illness with no clear end in sight.

'They can't see what's going on, it's invisible. Even if they could they probably don't know how to help you so you have to tell them. To the right people, you actually have to say, "I feel, I need, I want, and when I'm having a bad week, do you mind if I call you? Sometimes I just need to hear your voice and have a cry about it." If they're a true friend then they will have no issue with this whatsoever.'

The idea sounded so simple, yet I froze in fear. At the mere thought of asking for help my voice felt trapped, unable to make its way out. I knew I couldn't say those words. I worried that expressing such needs would be expecting too much from others, or they may feel obligated. I had experienced moments that left me feeling ashamed or let down when I reached out and there was no follow-up. No matter how much I could see what Heidi was saying was true, the block holding me back was like a giant concrete boulder. Too embarrassed to admit my reluctance, I remained silent.

'Vulnerability is imperative to get where we want to go. This is where we grow. You need to be willing to risk vulnerability. Start with the people you feel safe and supported with.'

Throughout the course, I came to realise the damaging impact of my own self-talk. Despite my efforts to combat limiting beliefs and self-judgement, my critical self-talk persisted, hampering my attempts at self-improvement.

In one of our sessions, I voiced my frustrations at my persistent inner critic. 'I recognise the harshness in the way I speak to myself, but no matter what I do, I can't seem to shift it,' I confessed.

'Losing your mum, there's no-one like a mother to soften life, to make you feel okay. It requires a lot of affirmations and reassurance,' Heidi explained. 'If you're not getting it elsewhere, you need to give it to yourself, and that requires being kind to yourself. It requires self-compassion, not this harshness.'

Immediately, tears welled up in my eyes at the reminder of the loss of my mother. The pain of grief, pushed aside and left unresolved, sat like a heavy rock in the pit of my stomach. I struggled to contain my emotions, choking back tears as I nodded in agreement. I missed the softness of my mother, her gentle presence. *If only she was still here, things would be different. Her presence and gentleness alone would help get me through.* But she isn't here, and her absence is a void I carry with me every day.

'One of the blocks to balancing your mind is your self-talk, being hard on yourself. Compassion requires you to have a loving relationship with yourself. You need to learn the art of self-love,' she said. 'The punching gloves have to come off.' I was my own worst critic, constantly berating myself and lacking self-compassion.

The program placed a significant emphasis on establishing a balanced foundation for living our dream lives. We delved into tools for nurturing a balanced mind, soul and overall life. One key task involved providing a detailed breakdown of our weekly schedules and analysing how we spent our time each day.

I was immediately confronted by the stark contrast between my reality and envisioned dream life. Despite striving to devote 20% of my time to soul-enriching pursuits and 80% to daily demands, my time and energy were disproportionately focused. Meaningful connections and soul-nourishing experiences were receiving little attention or energy.

This imbalance (dominated as it was by health-related commitments) left little room for activities to feed my soul. My deepest desire was to spend more time connecting with others. Seeing this disparity on paper was a sobering experience, highlighting the need for change.

'Stop striving. Focus on simply being. You've been in a learning phase, settling into a new way of being after enduring significant stress and trauma. You've acquired a wealth of new information and tools, and now it's time to embrace a period of learning to simply exist and grow, rather than always striving and doing.' It was true, I had been working so hard to improve my health I had lost myself in a battle where change seemed almost impossible.

Heidi's words resonated deeply, cutting through the noise of my constant striving. I had indeed been on a tireless quest for improvement, pushing myself to the brink in pursuit of better health. 'There's a part of you which needs to be reminded you have a choice to have your dream life whenever you want it. You don't need to keep denying yourself. Your recovery doesn't need to be so hard or so much work,' she remarked, her tone gentle yet firm.

I felt a flash of resistance. How could I embrace such a notion when my days were consumed by appointments and treatments, each one critical in the relentless battle against pain and suffering? Every moment, was a conscious decision to fight for my life, to cling to the hope of relief, no matter how fleeting it seemed.

Every week unfolded with an ongoing parade of specialists: dentists, neurologists, speech pathologists, pain psychologists, ENTs, pain physicians, facial surgeons, physiotherapists, acupuncturists, naturopaths, integrative doctors, craniosacral therapists, my GP. The roster of healthcare professionals seemed endless, but each played a pivotal role in addressing the multifaceted nature of my health challenges. Unfortunately, despite their expertise, healing remained elusive. My symptoms morphed and multiplied faster than we could keep up. In this ceaseless struggle, there was little room for anything beyond survival. No space for choice and certainly no respite from the unrelenting march of time.

Deep down, I knew Heidi was right. I had become so entrenched in the cycle of treatments I had forgotten the power of choice, the possibility of reclaiming my life beyond the confines of pain. But fear held me back, fear of letting go and surrendering to the unknown, fear the pain would consume me if I dared to loosen my grip, and fear I would fail to improve my life and be judged a failure.

As I sat with her message, the sobering realisation hit me, one which forced me to confront the harsh reality of my situation. *Had my tireless pursuit of recovery become another form of exertion, mirroring the same patterns of striving and struggle which had brought me to this point?* Despite my best intentions, I found myself trapped in the cycle of perpetually chasing after an elusive cure. But in doing so, I had lost sight of the true essence of healing – the simple act of being, of allowing myself to exist and grow without the pressure of constant effort and striving.

A quiet realisation began to take shape. Perhaps there was another way – a path of acceptance and surrender, where healing could unfold naturally, free from the constraints of relentless effort and struggle. It was a notion contrary to everything I had come to believe about recovery and everything I knew about approaching a challenge.

Towards the end of the course, we embarked on a deeper exploration of our values, aiming to identify the top five principles which would guide us in creating the life we desired. We examined which ones we were moving towards and which ones we were moving away from. Relationships and connections with others ranked among my highest values, aligning with the fundamental human need for connection. Isolated and alone, many of my days lacked the meaningful connections I craved.

With my ultimate goal of fostering meaningful connections in mind, I confronted the challenge of making space to prioritise these relationships. Questions filled my mind: *Where could I carve out time? What could I let go of to conserve energy for nurturing these connections? How could I overcome my fears of feeling like an obligation or facing rejection?*

Our final task involved identifying and tackling every obstacle standing in the way of achieving our desired life, whether related to relationships, time, health or finances. Under Heidi's guidance, we devised strategies to address each barrier. For me, these strategies ranged from having difficult conversations, scheduling appointment-free days, and gaining a comprehensive understanding of our financial situation. Post-shingles, this had changed significantly. The costs associated with managing my condition, coupled with having no superannuation building for retirement, forced me to confront the ongoing uncertainty of my circumstances.

While expenses continued to mount, staying alive and finding a way to live remained my top priority. Other life goals had to be relinquished, which carried enormous guilt. The one item I knew was at risk of being sacrificed was our beach shack at Smoky Bay, but neither John nor I could face making that decision. I couldn't bear the responsibility of losing it.

Armed with a blank calendar and a set of coloured markers representing my core values, I embarked on laying the groundwork for a more balanced existence. Prioritising at least one appointment-free day emerged as a crucial step, creating space for meaningful connections and activities unrelated to my health. Summoning courage, despite my loss of confidence and fear of rejection, I reached out to a handful of friends who I hoped might have time in their weekdays, tentatively proposing monthly catchups.

Among these friends, one in particular had been a constant support from the moment I contracted shingles and a lifeline during my darkest moments. In times of vulnerability, she held space for me in my pain, offering comfort through tears, frustration and loneliness. With each interaction, she always had the right words to say, adeptly validating my experiences while also challenging negative thoughts and beliefs. She was the one who during a check-in call, I voiced the fear I had been carrying – the terrifying thought I couldn't continue any longer. Within 24 hours I had received a crisis call and a beautiful arrangement of flowers arrived with the words, 'Life is beautiful.' She never failed to remind me how loved I was. When I proposed regular meetups, she eagerly embraced the idea. Her suggestion to sleep over at their home once a month on one of the nights John was at the mine, reduced me to tears. My plan included taking dinner, a gesture combining contribution with connection. However, as our plans unfolded, ignoring my protests, she insisted on taking care of dinner arrangements, knowing the drive was enough on its own.

Next, I reached out to another close friend I shared common interests with. Thoughtful and kind, she often reminded me how brave I was. Dialling her number nervously, I felt the familiar pang of fear, and worried about imposing on her time. With our shared passion for photography in mind, I tentatively proposed regular meetups to explore our mutual interest. To my relief, her enthusiastic response reassured me, and we soon found ourselves embarking on occasional photography outings. This conversation also led to the invitation to join a crafting group every second Friday when I felt able. This would provide another avenue for connection and an opportunity to knit in company rather than home alone. Though I worried pain might derail plans and my hearing might challenge me in larger groups, I felt a wave of relief at her response.

Weather permitting, I also enjoyed spontaneous walks on weekends with another close friend. Even though our arrangements happened naturally and organically, we usually made it work every few weeks. I attended social gatherings when I could, and sat back when communication fatigue set in. Along with the weekends John was away, weekdays proved my greatest challenge, so this became my focus moving forward. Managing my pain had begun to feel like a career and I wanted to shift away from this where I could.

As I reflected on my progress during the 12-week program, I still couldn't shake the persistent fear of rejection. Despite the myriad tools and support systems I had diligently put in place, these fears continued to loom large. I couldn't shake them. In our final session, Heidi offered a suggestion which sparked hope: 'I wonder if you should see a kinesiologist. I think there's something more going on here. Something beyond what we can get to.'

It wasn't the first time kinesiology had been suggested. Intrigued and willing to explore any avenue holding the promise of breakthrough, I heeded her advice and began researching kinesiologists in Adelaide and found one located only 10 minutes away. I held great respect for Heidi's knowledge, trusting her opinion and grateful for her holistic approach to healing. Her guidance had been instrumental in my journey so far.

Farewelling Heidi, I clung to the words of a quote from Matt Baker she had chosen for me, 'She never seemed shattered; to me, she was a breathtaking mosaic of the battles she's won.' I found solace in these affirming words which reminded me of my resilience and strength, in spite of the challenges I faced. While my time with Heidi had come to an end, I knew there was still work to be done on my path towards healing. Armed with the lessons learnt and the support I had gathered along the way, I felt a renewed sense of determination to continue pressing forward, one step at a time.

22.

THE BODY KEEPS SCORE

'We have learned that trauma is not just an event that took place sometime in the past; it is also the imprint left by that experience on mind, brain and body. This imprint has ongoing consequences for how the human organism manages to survive in the present.'
Bessel A. van der Kolk

The day of my first appointment with the kinesiologist finally arrived. I was filled with apprehension as I sat in yet another waiting room, pondering what lay ahead. There was no specific preparation required for the appointment – no reports to bring along, no tests to undergo, no results to anticipate. I wasn't entirely sure what to expect. *What was I here for?* I chuckled to myself, amused at my naivety. *I guess it's worth a shot.* Feeling stuck despite my efforts, I had been intrigued by the suggestion there might be something else going on. Another acquaintance had mentioned kinesiology could help release emotional blockages, unlocking feelings you may not even know you have. Research had hinted at a potential reduction in pain and improved energy, which was enough incentive for me to explore it further.

Breaking the silence, I heard, 'Denise,' in a lovely British accent. Looking up, I saw a smiling face full of warmth and kindness. As we walked the passage together, I instantly felt comfortable, her company somehow emanating a soothing presence. Falling into conversation with ease, she soon asked, 'How can I help you today?'

'I don't actually know,' I replied, feeling out of my depth. 'I've had several people suggest I see a kinesiologist but I'm not sure how you can help.' I went on to briefly explain my current circumstances, describing my journey with shingles and the subsequent ongoing pain. She listened attentively, acknowledging my challenging circumstances.

'Well, let's get you up on the bed and see what this body can tell us.'

As I lay on the bed, she proceeded with her assessment. Suddenly, she lifted her hands off me and remarked, 'You've got a lot of trauma in your body, girl. I can't get to the face pain until we clear it, so let's get to work, shall we?'

Continuing with her initial assessment, she detailed specific ages, down to the precise year and month, linked to traumatic events I had experienced throughout my life. Not fully understanding kinesiology, the revelations were unexpected. Bewildered by her pinpoint accuracy, I felt exposed as I immediately identified significant life events matching each age.

At the end of the assessment, age two came up. Confused, I replied, 'I don't have any clue. I've no knowledge of anything unusual then. I do remember feeling lost as a child. I don't remember a time I didn't feel it. Like I was alone.' Frowning, I tried to recall anything I heard or any major events in our life at that time. 'My brother was born just after I turned two. Maybe Mum had post-natal depression?' I wondered aloud. I was very attached to my mother, but I had always wanted to feel more connected with her. Even when I started playing netball, I recall hanging onto her skirt and not wanting to leave her side to go on the court. 'I don't know. My brother's birth is all that comes to mind,' I surmised, brushing it aside, believing she had this one wrong.

Shaking her head, she immediately responded emphatically, 'No, it's much more than that.'

At the end of our session, gently tapping my arm, she said, 'You need to stop saying no to you. It's time to add some joy in your life.' These were words I had heard before. Heidi had told me, the pain psychologist had told me. Thankfully, our holiday in the warmth was just around the corner. It would be just the thing to inject some much-needed happiness into my life.

It wouldn't be until six months later that I discovered more about the traumatic event linked to age two. I was speaking on the phone with a friend and during our conversation, I enquired about her husband, who had recently experienced a bout of pneumonia. Much like me, he had faced multiple recurrent episodes of pneumonia. In the midst of our discussion, she divulged his recurrent pneumonia can be traced back to having scarlet fever as a child. My eyes widened in surprise. 'You're kidding,' I said. 'I had scarlet fever as a child. I wasn't aware there was a connection. I wonder if that's what caused my lungs to be so sensitive to allergens? If I ever went near a cat, I'd be in hospital with pneumonia within days. Every time.'

Suddenly, a memory emerged. Recalling stories my parents had shared, I believed I was two or three years old when I had contracted scarlet fever. After hanging up, I immediately called my father and asked, 'Dad, how old was I when I had scarlet fever?'

'We'd just had Paul, so you were a bit over two I suppose. We had no idea where you got it from.'

'Did I go to hospital when I had it?' I asked, my stomach squirming, filled with dread at the thought I had been left alone in the hospital at such a young age.

'No. You had to stay home. It's contagious. We had to keep you away from the others. We couldn't let them get it, so you stayed in your room,' he explained.

Confused, I pressed for more details, 'What do you mean?'

'Well, we had to keep you isolated from the rest of the family. We had a newborn, and we couldn't risk exposing him to scarlet fever, so you stayed in your room for two weeks until you weren't contagious anymore. I brought your food in, and I'd come in the morning and again at night to put calamine all over you. You were covered in a rash from head to toe,' he recounted.

A sickening feeling surged through my entire body, followed by a sudden chill. *Locked in my room for two weeks? At only two years old?*

Shocked, I asked, 'How did I stay in there?'

'We put a bolt on your door. We had to stop the others getting it.'

The bolt. The frightening bolt, its presence looming over me throughout my entire childhood. The bolt at the top of the sliding door to my bedroom I had never understood. The bolt, its only purpose, as I saw through a child's eyes, to threaten confinement. The bolt that reminded me every night I went to bed it had the potential to lock me away.

'Did I cry? I asked, unsure if I wanted the answer.

'Cry? Oh, did you cry. You screamed blue bloody murder.' There was a long silence. 'You have no idea what we went through,' my father choked. Hearing his distress, I couldn't ask anything further.

Shocked, I struggled to process this new information. Heidi was right. There was something else going on, hindering my progress. The kinesiologist was right. It *was* something significant. My mind flooded with images of me as a little girl locked in her room for so long, in pain. At just two years of age, I had no way of understanding why I couldn't have my mother near me, why I had to be alone and couldn't be nurtured and cared for through illness and pain, why my family remained together yet I had to stay away. All I could have known was the aching loneliness, the absence of comfort, and the confusion of being kept apart from the people who were meant to soothe and comfort me.

Much later, in my healing journey, new understandings of my fears and behaviours gradually surfaced. Over time, I began to unravel the root cause of these, as my mind and body became more receptive to the process. This exploration even shed light on seemingly unrelated aspects of my life, such as my fear of closed doors in our home and my tendency to leave the bathroom door open so I could still hear and speak with my family. 'Mum, shut the door,' they would call out. Not understanding why I couldn't, I attempted humour in my responses. Often, I would laughingly call out, 'But then I can't talk to you.' I could enter tiny caves, crawl through tiny tunnels and be comfortable in many confined places, but I could not be in any small room where doors could be locked.

Reflecting on the homes we had purchased or built, I realised they often included an unusually large master bedroom. I had wondered why it seemed such an important feature. In homes where the room was smaller, the door would never be closed. The tiny bedroom I shared with my sister during childhood provided little space to move about and I had never felt comfortable being in there as a child. No doubt it had subconsciously represented a place of confinement rather than a place of rest. Solitude. Something I had never enjoyed and actively avoided. Now it was my new norm. It contrasted sharply with my need for company and connection. I was finally revealing the origins of a deep-seated fear.

Refusing to rest in my bedroom during the day had puzzled me for years. I always chose to rest on the couch with others around me. Now, with new-found clarity, I understood. I began to place more trust in the insights coaches and therapists had shared over the last two years.

I was beginning to see that each personal experience, no matter how difficult, held the potential to offer valuable lessons and perspectives that could shape my understanding of myself and the world around me.

As I embarked on this intriguing ongoing exploration of self-discovery and healing, I remained open to the possibility of finding meaning and purpose. Perhaps, amidst my struggles, I would uncover truths that would illuminate my path forward and bring me a sense of peace and acceptance.

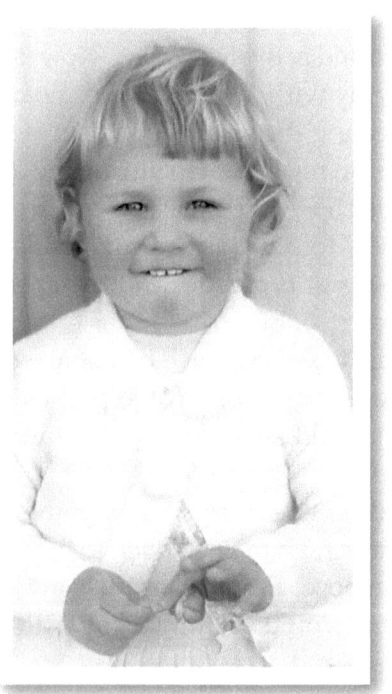

Just prior to scarlet fever

23.

TIME OUT

'I do things at pain levels others wouldn't even consider moving at because if I don't, I won't have a life. This doesn't mean I'm having a "good day". It only means that I was able to be stronger than the pain for part of the day.'
Author Unknown

By July, I was in the midst of my third winter living with the aftermath of shingles. I was eager to escape the frosty weather. For over two years I had depended on the warmer months to ease my fiery nerves. I could now focus on our August summer holiday to Europe, fitting in a whirlwind of appointments to prepare me for the trip. Braving the descent downstairs to our cold living space, I sat down and opened my laptop. Whether indoors or outdoors, there seemed no escape from the constant chill in the air. As I contemplated our holiday plans, a nagging concern resurfaced, *How will I navigate the air vents on the cruise ship?* It's one thing to sidestep them in everyday life, but another when they're an inescapable fixture of your surroundings. It was difficult enough managing air from the vents in our car on a short drive.

Gazing out at the dreary weather, I sighed at the lingering grip of winter. 'August can't come soon enough,' I shared with John the week before. Winter seemed to stretch on endlessly, a challenging and isolating time for me. Restricted to the confines of my home, I diligently worked on my mindset to keep my spirits up through long days. Heidi's suggestion of focusing on fun, adventure and freedom from appointments during our holiday sounded like the antidote I needed. I desperately yearned for a dose of fun.

Staring at our holiday documents on the screen, a knot tightened in my chest. After the latest blow, I needed to step away from my life more than ever. Just last week, another neurosurgeon assessed my condition and had described it as one of the most severe cases of PHTN he had encountered. He also indicated that without a response to some high-risk intervention, improvement was improbable. My state was likely to be permanent.

Although I had heard these words before, I desperately wanted words which held more hope. However, while it was devastating to hear, it also validated my experience. *I'm not imagining it. This is incredibly difficult. It's real.* Was I deluded then in thinking I could cope with an overseas holiday? To manage my condition each day in full public view? Regardless, I needed to escape the cold. With no medication to rely on, I had to explore other avenues and a warmer climate offered a small but consistent source of relief.

With only weeks to go until departure, I marked another day off the calendar. My friend and I were both turning 50 this year, so it was our turn to choose a holiday destination to celebrate with our friends. She had been a wonderful support, particularly in my first six months after shingles, regularly spending time with me on a Sunday despite her exhausting week of work. Without fail, she phoned every week, always thoughtful of how alone I might feel during John's absence.

When she suggested a Mediterranean cruise, the mere thought of 14 days in the warmth of the Greek Islands was enough to convince me it was both a great idea and an achievable holiday. With my situation as it stood, I felt deeply honoured to be holidaying with friends to celebrate. John and I had opted to extend our time in the warmth and cruise Croatia together for an additional part of my celebration. Two other couples decided they would love to join us also, giving me even more to look forward to.

When the holiday was first raised, John and I had discussed at length how we could approach the trip to minimise the impact on me. 'It's going to be a significant jump to go from long days at home alone to full days of socialising. There'll be a lot more talking and laughing no doubt, so I'll have constant triggers to my face. Obviously, eating is worrying me,' I had shared, as we discussed possible implications. I knew I would need downtime on my own and rest time in my days. 'I'm worried about the food situation but I'm more worried about sleep. It can become unmanageable if I don't get sleep.'

Nodding gently, his reply had offered reassurance. 'There will be plenty of options for soft food on the cruise and there's always soup. Just rest when you can in the afternoons. If you're not up to the shore excursions, don't go. I won't object to a rest in the afternoon.'

Still only able to manage two to four hours sleep each night, I had learnt to function on whatever I could get. With so many potential environmental triggers, additional sleep deprivation would be highly likely. Tiredness would impact what I could do but worse still, it led to increased pain. In company all day, this would be difficult if I couldn't manage it. However, seeing so many new places for the first time, I also felt hopeful the sights would offer some welcome distraction.

John was aware of the careful planning required and often the one prompting me to make adjustments if I needed. Sometimes, when he noticed me pushing myself too hard, he would gently remind me of the consequences. At times I overheard him explaining to friends when they shared their joy at witnessing me enjoying activities, 'Yes, but it comes with a price. She'll pay for it later.' Despite this, he understood the need for balance and never discouraged me.

By early August, the weather in Adelaide was bitterly cold. Struggling with the temperatures and the isolation, I boarded the plane with a mixture of apprehension and excitement. Regardless of my concerns, I was eager to escape winter and enjoy being in company. Thanks to accumulated Qantas points, I had secured a business class seat. I was doing everything possible to make the flight manageable.

Having my own cubicle on the flight allowed me to control the airflow in my immediate area and provided the opportunity to lie and rest. While the take-offs and landings were difficult to manage, once we reached cruising altitude, the additional discomfort subsided.

On arrival in Germany, I was greeted by perfect weather conditions: minimal wind and temperatures between 26 and 28 degrees Celsius every day. The climate soon helped reduce the intensity of my pain. I seized every opportunity to spend time outdoors, taking breaks to rest in the afternoons or having lay days at our friends' home.

Our time together was a wonderful blend of relaxation and exploration, as we visited places I had only dreamt of seeing. My hosts proved the perfect travel companions and were aware of my need to manage fatigue. They had long embraced the benefits of a relaxed approach to travel, a skill I struggled to master but adopted during our adventures together. Managing my situation with photography and rest days, I found overwhelming joy in what I was able to achieve without significantly impacting our travel plans. While the pain remained an enduring companion, the warm weather and the relief from constant decision-making and appointments were welcomed changes in my daily routine. Decision-making fatigue had set in long ago, and my friends' thoughtful and considered plans for our time together reduced my mental load. It provided a welcome reprieve each day and positively impacted my energy levels. Being in the company of others, immersed in vastly different daily life experiences and surroundings, lifted the sombre mood that had lingered throughout the winter months.

After six weeks, we farewelled each other when we met up with John and our friends in Croatia. I was acutely aware the next leg of my holiday would be more active and offer less time for solitary rest. No longer a backseat passenger in a quiet car of three, but on a cruise, I knew I would have less control over my surroundings. My hearing immediately presented a significant challenge indoors in a large group. With additional background noise, every sound reverberated through me, appearing much louder than usual and sending my ear pain skyrocketing. Combined with distorted sounds and voices, it made listening challenging and exhausting. It required intense focus. With less opportunity to escape conversation to allow my mind rest, at times I found it difficult to conceal my struggles. Despite this, I summoned courage and smiled through, determined to remain engaged.

Our first cruise took us through the stunning waters of Croatia. My dietary restrictions were accommodated impeccably. There were moments when I glanced at the menu, longing to enjoy the dishes served to others, to blend in seamlessly and not draw attention to my needs. However, the desire to try the meals that required more chewing was quickly overtaken by the fear of potential repercussions and the uncertainty of whether I could even swallow the food.

Bathed in warmth, I soaked in the simple joy of being outdoors. The sense of freedom it brought was indescribable, almost surreal. One evening, during the early stages of the cruise, I confided in John, 'I wish we'd been able to leave Australia six weeks earlier. It's so much easier to manage in the warmth. I can feel tiredness affecting me and wish I could get more sleep, but I'm warm. Taking photos is helping a lot. I can't believe I'm actually doing this to be honest. I never thought I'd make it this far,' I disclosed, my eyes filling with tears as I reflected on how hard I worked to keep pushing through.

'You're doing really well,' he said.

In spite of mounting exhaustion and the increasing intensity of my pain, each day I armed myself with my camera, determined to distract myself and maintain a positive presence. Often, I pushed my limits but when I could, I sought refuge in the warmth on the back deck or took a short break in my room. These moments gave my face relief from the interactions that fuelled my pain.

After farewelling our friends at the end of the Croatian cruise, I felt a renewed determination to maintain my positive outlook each day, knowing the next two weeks would be just John and I. It would provide much needed time to rest my face and recharge before we met up with friends again for our Mediterranean cruise.

We embarked on our relaxing week in Santorini, followed by eight wonderful days in Positano. While we had chosen a night to celebrate my birthday in every location we visited, Positano held special significance because we would be there on the actual day. After the onset of PHTN, not a day had gone by when I truly believed I would live to see this day. It would be a special moment for me on our holiday.

On the day of my birthday, our day trip to Capri was cancelled due to rough sea conditions. Instead, we spent the day wandering the streets, enjoying local art and shops, and time lying under the beach umbrellas. Deciding it would be appropriate to purchase an outfit for my 'celebration of life' on return home, we searched for a special dress. As we wandered, I often found myself in a state of disbelief. I became distinctly aware of how close I had come to missing all of this, never walking these streets or any street again, never experiencing another sunrise or sunset. Worst of all, not seeing my beautiful girls blossom through life with John beside me. Silent tears fell on and off throughout the day. Tears of enduring unimaginable pain, of desperate sadness, of indescribable loss, of deep shame, of profound fear, mixed with tears of happiness, joy and survival. In the flood of emotions, it proved difficult to pinpoint how I truly felt.

I continued shedding happy tears throughout our week in Positano, particularly during the long hikes I had included in our plans, uncertain they would ever eventuate. From December in 2017, I had marked each day in my nine-month countdown toward 50 as another day surviving life. Another day still pushing on, still showing up, even though I desperately wanted something, anything, to end my pain and suffering. It was deeply painful to acknowledge I had often wished for life to end to find relief. Perhaps it wasn't surprising to feel this way, given how often such sentiments were shared in the TN support group. Yet here I was. I had reached 50 having endured what many believed to be unendurable. I was still standing. I had made it.

TIME OUT

Departing Positano, we were excited to meet up with our friends in Tuscany for a few days before setting sail on our cruise. Despite my excitement, an undercurrent of apprehension still remained. Acutely aware of the challenge to disguise my pain over long periods, I would need to find a way to include rest breaks in a way that wouldn't dampen our collective experiences. I had no choice. My desire to be fully engaged in evening cruise entertainment experiences would require careful planning and pacing throughout each day but I knew I would make it work even if I had to miss out on activities.

'I wish I could wake up and not have to meticulously plan every aspect of my day, from what I eat to when I rest. It's so frustrating,' I confided in John part way through the cruise. Unlike our experience on the Croatian cruise, we lacked control over the air-conditioning in our rooms. Nights, already difficult, became even more challenging with the continuous oscillating cool air on me. With only two to three hours of sleep each night, I operated in survival mode each day.

'I know it's not easy,' John replied, understanding evident in his voice. 'It's not easy seeing you go through it either.'

I nodded, feeling the weight of exhaustion pressing down on me. 'It's like fighting a battle against my own body.'

Growing increasingly self-conscious and worn out, I began to face each day with a sense of weariness. 'Are you okay?' John asked, his brow furrowing with concern as we disembarked for another day of exploration.

'I'm really tired today,' I replied, forcing a smile to mask my unease. 'But I want us to make the most of it.'

Together, we made a concerted effort to enjoy each morning in a new port, taking shore excursions to explore the islands.

Early in the cruise, we discovered the local cuisine often didn't cater to my dietary needs, predominantly offering meat dishes with limited options for softer or liquid-based foods. This meant we maximised our time exploring the islands in the mornings before returning to the ship to seek out suitable meals and steal moments of rest.

Finding the air-conditioning intolerable in our room, I found solace in the warmth around the pool in the afternoons. I relished quiet moments of respite to recharge before the evening's social engagements. Despite the difficulties, I remained determined to make the most of our cruise experience, cherishing the moments of joy and camaraderie.

One day, after failing to manage my pain well through the day, I gave in. During the cocktail evening the six of us had signed up for, I allowed myself a few drinks.

'You know you're going to pay for this,' John remarked gently during the event, his concern evident in his voice.

His honest expression of my reality was heartbreaking, yet his understanding brought comfort. 'I know, but my face isn't great today anyway, so what difference does it make?' I replied with resignation.

Allowing myself the joy of singing along at the piano bar with others, it felt liberating despite the immediate shocks that tore through my face and ear as soon as I began singing. As it intensified through the evening, I continued to share in the experience, refusing to let it bring my evening to an abrupt end. I cherished the opportunity to join our friends in the fun.

However, the combination of triggers proved too much. Eventually, I retreated to our room, tears falling as I entered. I had held them back for the last two hours, managing to smile and laugh through the night. I'd had fun, but the toll of putting on a brave face was undeniable.

Restless throughout the night, sleep eluded me, exacerbated by John's snoring. I had pushed myself too far. Distressed by my suffering and inability to fall asleep, he retreated to sleep in the bathroom, a sight that left me devastated when I discovered him there in the middle of the night. Insisting he return to bed, I vowed to manage myself better in future.

Physically, I managed some wonderful shore excursion walks with John or with our friends, often making our way to the highest buildings or to the top of forts to experience stunning panoramic views of each location. But while I handled the physical demands of shore excursions, what I hadn't fully anticipated was the mental fatigue accompanying daily socialising and its cumulative toll on my face. Navigating the delicate balance was exhausting. On shore, my camera remained my trusted ally, providing both a shield to hide behind and short respites from conversation. Though not without its flaws, my strategies – afternoon rests, watching what I ate and photography – allowed me to enjoy being with friends while taking in the sights at each new port. While there were moments when I drifted into my own world, battling against my pain, John discreetly kept me moving forward.

'You can stay on shore if you don't want to come back to the boat with me,' I shared with John one day, not wanting him to feel obligated to join me.

'I know, but I'm happy with what we're doing. I've seen everything I want to by then, plus I enjoy relaxing on the boat in the afternoon. We don't have to be doing things all the time.'

Arriving in the Cinque Terre after farewelling our friends in Venice at the end of the cruise, I stood in awe of the incredible view in front of us. 'John, I can hardly believe I'm here. I knew it wouldn't be easy, but I'm doing it,' I shared, overwhelmed with gratitude for the experience.

Sleeping better without air constantly blowing on me overnight, I slowly recovered from the cruise and regained energy for the final week of our holiday.

As we returned home, preparing to celebrate life with close friends and family, I couldn't help but smile. Not only had I made it to 50, I had managed an overseas holiday, defying my own expectations and embracing life in ways I never thought possible.

Sitting to write a speech for my party, overwhelming emotions poured out. This wasn't a celebration of age milestone, it was a celebration of life, of survival, of resilience, of the sheer determination to keep going in spite of the odds. It was a chance to express gratitude to those who had been my pillars of support, who had turned up in any small way. It was a chance to thank those who had stood by me through the darkest of times, through the ongoing struggle, and through the tireless pursuit of normalcy.

It was an opportunity to acknowledge the unwavering friendships that had weathered the storm, regardless of the changes my journey had brought in how I showed up in their lives. While I celebrated my birthday overseas, some had been busy at home planning and pouring their love and creativity into every detail of the celebration. In preparation, a small group of friends decorated our home. Our outdoor area was adorned with my favourite quotes, words that had carried me through the toughest moments, all framed and neatly inscribed in white paint. They transformed the space with countless jars of exquisite white flowers and lush greenery, filling our home with a sense of beauty and renewal. John had the backyard looking impeccable. Our daughter had lovingly created playlists of my favourite music and together our girls prepared a magnificent grazing table. Along with my husband and two daughters, 45 beautiful people shared in the night of celebration with heartfelt loving speeches delivered throughout the evening. I had made it. It was the end of 2018 and I had made it.

Reaching 50
Sketch – A gift from my girls
John and I celebrating

24.

MORE LOSS

*'Health is like money; we never have
a true idea of its value until we lose it.'*
Josh Billings

As the new year unfolded, its path soon revealed itself to me. In January 2019, I found myself in the endodontist's chair, undergoing a procedure to remove nerves from a tooth near the site of my tangled, damaged nerves. My pain had reached unbearable levels. It was during this time I encountered the oral and maxillofacial surgeon whose incredible insights shed light on the pervasive nature of living with PHTN. The frustration of seeking understanding in a world that often fails to recognise such struggles seemed to be a universal challenge. Despite outward appearances of wellness, the true extent of my suffering remained hidden. Only those closest to me could detect the subtle shifts in behaviour that silently echoed the ongoing internal battle; the forgetfulness, sudden onset of mental fatigue, glazed eyes, loss of focus in conversations and the struggle to keep up with daily self-care.

As my short-term memory continued to fail me, its impact became increasingly disruptive. In February, acknowledging the severity of the situation, I undertook a comprehensive evaluation with a neuropsychologist. The purpose was to determine the nature and severity of cognitive dysfunction and pinpoint the root cause of my memory struggles.

As I made my way to the neuropsychologist's office for my first appointment, I felt a rush of shame. My thoughts were clouded by reflections on how my faltering memory had gradually worn down my confidence. The myriad reactions to my memory challenges over the past three years had taken a toll on my self-esteem. Often, my family's responses were tinged with frustration whenever I failed to recall information they shared, or I had unwittingly repeated questions. Annoyance for what seemed like inattentiveness often left me in a state of agitation, further hindering my ability to concentrate and retain information. Despite my efforts to remember, it felt as though the details were sucked into a void, beyond my reach. Occasionally, I sensed the frustration of friends when I forgot things, but most approached the situation with humour. They good-naturedly retrieved forgotten items and reminded me of special dates.

Arriving at my appointment, I was met with a warm friendly welcome from the neuropsychologist. Her thoughtful questioning and empathetic responses immediately put me at ease, validating the frustrations I had been experiencing. After a thorough discussion to gather relevant information, she proposed a plan: 'Given your circumstances, I think we'll do the assessment over three appointments to give the best chance of an accurate result.' Grateful for her understanding and consideration, I left the appointment, confident she would unravel the mysteries surrounding my memory issues.

Ironically, on the day of my scheduled appointment for the first assessment session, I arrived at the pain clinic instead. In the opposite direction and 25 minutes away from where I should have been. *My brain ... What would they discover?* Eventually arriving 15 minutes late, the investigation into my cognitive function finally began. The sessions proved both gruelling and confronting, rapidly uncovering the degree of memory impairment. Amidst the challenges, there was a moment of excitement when I believed I had successfully completed an entire task accurately, only to discover later it was a simple test of honesty in responses.

Results of my short-term memory test, ranking me in the extremely low range, highlighted significant memory issues. As devastating as the results were, it also validated my daily struggles. Finally, I had an explanation for the challenges I encountered in maintaining focus and attention during conversations or while watching a movie. It explained the reason behind my frequent memory lapses. Other aspects of the assessment clarified why activities like jigsaw puzzles, once a favourite pastime, had become an almost insurmountable challenge. Similarly, my attempts at scrapbooking, once a source of joy, now left me staring at a blank piece of card, unable to decipher where to begin or how to plan the page. This new knowledge also accounted for the sudden change in my decision-making abilities. It shed light on the difficulties I encountered in retaining information during the courses I had undertaken.

A follow-up brain MRI with a second neuropsychologist, confirmed initial thoughts. The unrelenting pain I endured was directly impacting my cognitive processes, namely memory and focus. Pain had hijacked my mind. His interpretation offered a glimmer of reassurance. 'I don't want you to think this is permanent; it's not. You just need to get the pain under control.' Even though I had no idea how I could do that, they were reassuring words I had been desperately hoping for.

Knowing I wasn't losing my mind or succumbing to the early stages of dementia was a relief. Instead, I was confronted with the harsh truth that pain was having an adverse influence on my cognition. It reshaped my understanding of my own limitations and challenges.

At this critical juncture, with my pain still uncontrolled, John and I faced a decision that had been looming over us for some time. With him away for work, the upkeep of our home had become a significant challenge for me. Its expansive size, complete with a swimming pool and large garden, demanded constant maintenance and cleaning – a task made increasingly daunting by my fatigue, memory lapses and balance issues. Despite the fact we had meticulously planned our home for the long term, we could no longer ignore that my health made its management untenable while he still worked away. It was a difficult decision but one we had ignored for too long in the hope things would improve.

The process of preparing and selling our home proved to be an emotional and physically draining ordeal, adding another loss to the continuously growing list. However, amidst our sadness, in our search for a more manageable home, we discovered a lovely light-filled townhouse with a modest garden only a short one-minute walk to the beachfront. Its convenient location perfectly aligned with our shared love of the ocean and the proximity to friends and the airport would prove invaluable, especially in facilitating John's FIFO travel. As generous friends helped pack up our home, set up our new kitchen and organised our clothes, I felt a mixture of both loss and relief. Despite having fewer responsibilities, and knowing we were making the right decision on many levels, I also recognised it would take time to come to terms with the bittersweet reality of our relocation.

25.

REGRESSION

'Your beliefs become your thoughts,
Your thoughts become your words,
Your words become your actions,
Your actions become your habits,
Your habits become your values,
Your values become your destiny.'
Gandhi

In the months following our move and throughout the remainder of 2019, we devoted ourselves to adding unique personal touches to our new space, which helped ease the emotions that came with missing aspects of our former home. Introducing elements of warmth, we replaced cold tiles with inviting wooden floorboards and refreshed the space with a coat of paint, bringing new life into our surroundings.

We quickly grew to love our light-filled home and I immediately benefited from the warmth it brought to the living spaces. The absence of the jarring shocks that once greeted me each morning as I descended the stairs in our previous home provided a welcome reprieve.

After completing the improvements in September, discussions about adding a dog to our family surfaced. It had been six years since we had lost our first dog, Mickey, and I longed for the unconditional love and companionship of another dog. However, John remained steadfast in his reluctance. 'Not yet. We can get one later,' he reiterated each time the conversation arose.

Although I craved the comforting presence of a dog, my ongoing struggles with memory issues cast a shadow of doubt over the topic. Apprehensive about my ability to care for a puppy, I feared I would forget to tend to its needs or lacked the necessary energy to keep up. My pain experience remained unchanged, each day blending into the next. Appointments still consumed much of my time and lack of sleep and fatigue remained stubbornly persistent. Despite these reservations, the companionship of a puppy was appealing.

Two months later, during a visit to the market, the conversation about welcoming a dog into our lives came up again. Our friends, passionate dog lovers themselves, eagerly voiced their support for the idea with genuine enthusiasm. Encouraged by their positive feedback, and perhaps a fun-loving hint of peer pressure, John finally relented. I wasted no time enquiring about availability with a cavoodle breeder in NSW I had been following for the past 18 months. Six weeks later, our eagerly anticipated new family member, Gracie, was enroute to join our family.

'What if she doesn't like me when I come home?' John shared with a grin as I dropped him at the airport for his return to work. Gracie would arrive the following day. 'She will, I know she will,' I reassured him with a smile. It had been a quick turnaround, and I could sense his hidden excitement about her imminent arrival, in spite of his initial reservations.

In early 2020, I eagerly made my way to the airport with a friend to welcome our newest addition, the calm and delightful ruby-red cavoodle, Gracie. If it's possible to fall in love with a dog at first sight, we certainly did. However, as I settled her into our home, the reality of caring for a new puppy quickly materialised.

I was abruptly reminded of the exhaustion that comes with puppy parenthood. I felt like I'd been hit by a freight train. Despite my ongoing need for significant rest throughout the day to combat fatigue, the demands of puppy care left little room for respite. Balancing hours in the kitchen preparing my meals and attending five or six appointments each week, I often collapsed into bed each night, overwhelmed by physical exhaustion and the added pain it brought.

While I had initially viewed getting a dog as a positive step, I hadn't fully anticipated the significant impact it would have on my already limited energy reserves. When John called one night asking, 'How's Gracie?' I fought back tears, sharing, 'She's so cute but I've never felt so fatigued in all my life. It's exhausting.' I chose not to divulge I had fallen over three times bending to pick her up, my loss of balance reminding me to make adjustments.

Laughing, he replied, 'I can't wait to see her.' I couldn't wait for him to come home to get to know her. Already bringing an abundance of joy to my life, I knew she was a wonderful addition to our family. Despite the challenging puppy stage, her companionship was an invaluable distraction. She also provided a welcome new topic of conversation and a new purpose.

Two months after Gracie arrived, our youngest daughter left Australia with plans to travel and work in the UK for two years. However, her plans were abruptly disrupted as Australia recorded its first case of community transmission of COVID the day before her departure. Within two weeks, she returned home as our borders closed. With her plans shattered, she moved back home and we did our best to lift her spirits while she worked out her next steps.

As the pandemic unfolded, Zoom emerged as a new way of connecting with loved ones. With my compromised lungs, I was cautioned to be extra vigilant, making difficult decisions to protect myself. Like many during the COVID pandemic, I faced criticism and judgement for my caution. At first, I wanted to defend my decisions, but I soon realised not everyone would understand that with my lowered immunity and compromised lungs, I had no choice. However, I was sensitive to comments and feared disappointing others, particularly at a time when my sense of connection to those around me felt more distant than ever. Once again, I felt confined within the walls of my own home. Our plans to escape to Europe for part of the winter were dashed, leaving me no respite from the cold season. My pain levels soared, my energy plummeted and my spirits sank low.

Over the past two years, I had never worked so hard on my mindset, acutely aware of the toll chronic pain takes on mental health and the amount of work required to keep on top of it. Despite this, my strength and resilience waned. *Have I made any progress?* I wondered. *Will I ever be resilient to criticism and judgement?* Thoughts came thick and fast, relentlessly invading my mind and sucking me back into the limiting beliefs Heidi had previously challenged me on.

With little to focus on, COVID restricting connections with others even further, and a holiday with friends in the warmth cancelled, I worked harder to put supports in place to lift my spirits. Feeling alone, I knew what to do and increased gratitude, affirmation, mindfulness and yoga practices, but still I could not stop a tirade of negative thoughts. The punching gloves were back on. Suddenly, I was at my lowest point with no reserves. Alone with my thoughts, alone in my home, alone with my pain. Alone in a COVID bubble, I plummeted.

26.

HEIDI RETURNS

'If we can share our story with someone who responds with empathy and understanding, shame can't survive.'
Brené Brown

Late in April 2020, John took time off work for our annual holiday at Smoky Bay. My mood was low and I struggled to bounce back despite my efforts. Immensely frustrated with a returned sense of failure and aloneness, feelings of shame and worthlessness intensified. I continued to feel lost, aimlessly drifting like a boat without anchor. Living each day exhausted, emotional upheaval added weight I had little energy to be resilient to.

During the long drive from Adelaide to Smoky Bay, John struggled to find the right words to say as I voiced the vulnerable words, 'I'm really struggling, John. I'm worried I can't get myself out of this. I've got nothing left in me. I'm fighting so hard to stay here but it's too hard. This is no life and on top of that, I'm either frustrating people or letting them down. I'm just tired. So tired.'

After a long pause, he placed his hand on my knee, 'You'll get through this.'

'No part of me feels like I will. I feel like a dead person walking. I don't have the energy to keep trying.' I replied, feeling utterly defeated. The weight of seeing John struggle, pained by his inability to find the right words, broke my heart. But this time, I felt depleted, as though I didn't have enough fight left, even for him or my girls. I desperately wanted to keep going for them, I just didn't feel I had enough to draw on. As their faces flashed through my mind, an unbearable ache returned at the thought of the pain my surrendering would inflict on them. Immediately I thought of Christmas day, only four months prior, when they had gifted me a box of over 50 little handmade cards they had made together. Each was lovingly inscribed with a special memory or something they appreciated about me – words every mother longs to hear. In the years that followed, those cards became a lifeline. Every time I opened one, I felt their love and presence despite their physical absence. Each card reduced me to tears, with heartfelt messages like, *'I have really lovely memories of you, me and Granny drinking tea and eating biscuits at the shack. I feel so lucky to have spent that time with you both,'* and *'We love your ability to push through when times are tough, and it inspires and encourages us to do the same.'* I desperately wanted to create more memories with them and for them.

Two hours into the trip, I had a lengthy call on the phone to a long-term friend. Unable to mask my despair any longer, I tearily shared the dark space I was in. Although I knew she was a safe, supportive and confidential friend with whom to share, it was frightening to voice my pain to someone.

Through heartbreaking sobs, I quietly shared, 'I'm done. I've truly had enough. I can't do this anymore. It's beaten me. I keep showing up smiling when I want to cry. I'm doing everything I can to make this easier for everyone. People don't see what I push myself through just to get up in the morning. I don't want to live with this ridiculous pain anymore. I feel like I'm just making life hard for everyone. It's crushed me.' I thought I had hit rock bottom many times over the past four years, but this time was different.

HEIDI RETURNS

This time, I was there. I felt it in every bone in my body. I could see it in my glazed hollow eyes.

We spoke between long periods of silence until it felt like neither of us could bear the pain of helplessness. Defeated on every level, I knew there was little anyone could do, and guilt had set in because I had shared a heavy load. Yet, an unspoken understanding existed in that moment – there was nothing I wanted from her, except to be heard, there was nothing she needed to do, except listen. She gifted me her understanding by remaining present to my sharing, compassionate in her responses. Her presence brought warmth and safety, and at that moment, I suddenly no longer felt alone in my internal pain.

A quiet resignation took place between us on that call. I'd spoken a painful truth, silenced for so long, now suddenly heard. Understood. Accepted. The flood gates had opened. It wasn't possible to hide anymore. Finally, I openly allowed myself to be seen, to be completely vulnerable. I hoped she could handle it and wouldn't abandon me. Feeling freedom I'd never experienced as I uttered each word, I bravely continued. I shared my deep inner world of emotional torment without holding back, as she courageously listened, validating my experience.

Those silent moments we shared gave rise to a new understanding. She would tell me as much later; it was only after that conversation she finally understood the full extent of living with PHTN and what I was dealing with. Calling me later that day to check on us, her quiet but powerful words stayed with me for our entire trip, 'Denise you hang on for those girls of yours. You're not alone. You are *not* alone. John, just keep hanging on to her.' John, with tears in his eyes, was equally grateful for her words of support, words he struggled to express amidst his own pain.

Arriving at Smoky Bay, I numbly cleaned Little Bet feeling I'd somehow detached from my body. Ironically, it was where I had contracted chickenpox as a toddler, the reactivated virus now threatening my existence. In a daze, I eventually curled up on the front bed in my mother's favourite spot, looking out to sea, and I wept. I wept for all I'd lost. I wept for the aloneness. I wept at the physical absence of my beautiful daughters and the impact on them. I wept for John. I wept for my friends and all they had lost. I wept unknowingly for what I would later understand to be the little girl waiting to be seen, heard and given words of comfort. I wept for my family. I wept for my childhood. I wept at my failed efforts to do my best. I wept.

As we sat and ate our tea that night, four years into my shingles battle, a heavy cloud hung over us, silence filling the unlined walls. Even the cheerfulness of the shack couldn't lift me. John, his love for me unmistakable, yet unsure of how to navigate emotional moments, busied himself by tidying up outside and preparing the boat.

That night, sleep eluded me. At 2 am, I gave up and picked up my phone to check my emails. Distracting myself from my thoughts, I began deleting and filing emails, a mindless administration task long overdue. In keeping with other miraculous life-changing interventions in my journey, what unfolded in the next 24 hours would prove to be one of the most profound turning points of my life.

Opening an email in my inbox about a health summit, I briefly scanned my eyes over it. It was starting the following day, and as I scrolled down, I suddenly noticed Heidi's photograph amongst the list of presenters. Curious, I read it thoroughly. Over four days, several well-known entrepreneurs from around the world would outline courses they were offering on various topics in response to COVID, covering aspects of health, finances and business. *I need a bit of Heidi. It worked last time.* Immediately registering, I put my phone down feeling some comfort in knowing I'd soon have contact with her.

27.

ILLUMINATE

*'Between stimulus and response there is a space.
In that space is our power to choose our response.
In our response lies our growth and our freedom.'*
Viktor Frankl

After barely two hours of sleep, I woke feeling exhausted, my eye engulfed in searing, grating pain. After applying drops to soothe it, I slowly made my way out of bed and opened the bedroom curtains. Standing in the kitchen, I caught sight of my reflection in the mirror and noticed the significant droop of my eyelid and the crooked way my mouth sat across my face. A stark reminder of my damaged nerves, confronting, undeniable and quite literally, etched across my face.

'John, my face isn't great today. Do you need me in the boat?' I asked, my voice heavy with fatigue.

'Your eye looks terrible,' John observed, glancing across the kitchen. 'I'm setting up the boat today so go back to bed and see if you can get some rest.'

While the exhaustion weighed me down, the idea of returning to bed held no appeal. No, today would be a day of knitting to distract myself while I waited for Heidi's workshop over Zoom.

Seeing Heidi's face appear on the screen that day was a welcome sight, even as I fought the overwhelming weight of hopelessness. Sensing I was embarking on the fight of my life, I desperately clung to the hope her program would provide the support I needed. Her wisdom, knowledge and ability to identify actionable steps offered me a quiet sense of possibility.

After four years of so much pain and loss, I was weary of the seemingly endless battle to maintain positive mental health amidst the ongoing upheaval. It felt like an insurmountable mission. As I stared at the screen, I felt frustrated at the futility of my efforts. *I have the tools, I do the work, yet still I struggle.*

This time, Heidi had collaborated with another coach to offer a program of holistic health called 'Illuminate'. Their program would cover every aspect of health, from toxicity to environment, hormones to nutrition, sleep to mindfulness, mindset to purpose. It promised a comprehensive approach to wellness, offering the possibility of relief and restoration over the course of three transformative months.

As Heidi delved into the program details, two key points resonated with me. Firstly, she emphasised the importance of simplicity in making health changes. 'When we embark on a journey to improve our health, it often feels like scaling an insurmountable mountain. But it doesn't have to be that way. We can keep it simple. By focusing on one key area that will have the greatest butterfly effect on every other aspect of our health, we can make significant progress. Most times, that area is stress.'

Living with chronic pain, trying to disguise the extent of my suffering, grappling with multiple losses and changes, and enduring the isolating nature of my condition, I was all too familiar with the need to manage stress.

Next, Heidi raised the importance of self-compassion. 'When we're under stress, it's crucial to learn the art of self-compassion. The first step is to recognise that the thoughts in our minds will never stop. Our minds are wired to keep us safe, to help us survive, striving to ensure our acceptance. This can be exhausting.' I felt every truth in her words as she continued, 'Buying into our thoughts will make us feel crap about ourselves.'

Exhaling, I acknowledged this was precisely where I found myself. 'These thoughts are just stories. They feel real because following thought is emotion, a feeling, and we buy into believing it's real because you have a feeling or sensation in your body that reinforces it,' she explained. I was desperate to stop the sensations attached to my thoughts.

'You have a choice to look at those thoughts and say, *That's not helpful. It's not going to help me become the person I want to be*,' Heidi continued. 'What we need to do is examine the thoughts and stories. The perceptions we have about the world, our lives and ourselves, that's where the stress begins.'

But I've tried. They are so ingrained I can't shift them no matter what. It's driving me mad. I wanted to scream. Despite my efforts, when confronted with judgement or criticism for not living up to expectations, I felt like I had committed a crime. *What's wrong with me? Why do I experience such an overwhelming sense of guilt at not measuring up?*

Later, I would come to uncover a deeply ingrained subconscious belief: that my worthiness of love and belonging was contingent upon doing things for others flawlessly. To never slip up. Keeping others happy, would somehow make me worthy of love if I'd performed well enough to earn it. It was as though their happiness and approval were the prerequisites for my own sense of belonging. This mindset knew no bounds; I felt compelled to fulfil others' needs at any cost, believing only then I would be loved and accepted. Even amidst illness, fatigue, pain and isolation, I felt an unyielding pressure to never let anyone down. There was no room for error. It was a suffocating existence, marked by a constant fear of falling short and the exhaustive weight of perfectionism.

'Not buying into the thought takes practice, but the mind loves repetition and habit,' Heidi explained. 'You can either take the thought and run with it, or you can simply notice it. Instead of trying to avoid it, control it, push it down or become entangled with it, ask yourself if it's helpful or not. Is it aligning with your values? Is it guiding you toward the person you want to be?'

I understood this concept intellectually, but I struggled to develop self-compassion around my thoughts. Instead, I fell into a pattern of relentless self-criticism.

'What we tend to do is put on our punching gloves and beat ourselves up for feeling that way. It's human nature. We start thinking, *There's something wrong with me. I'm not going to be accepted*,' she explained.

Heidi outlined the power of using breath to disrupt thoughts. She reminded us of the importance of bringing ourselves into the present to cultivate kindness and compassion towards ourselves, rather than perpetually beating ourselves up believing we're doing something wrong.

'It doesn't mean the story will go, but that interruption breath is enough to bring you into the present. You can't create out of chaos. In the present moment, you have the choice to act based on your values, the person you want to be and the vision you have for your life.'

Her words served as a reminder of the profound influence our minds have over us and the continuous effort needed to challenge and transform unhelpful beliefs. I was ready to take responsibility and break free from the patterns keeping me stuck.

'You need support. You can't do this on your own. No-one does self-development on their own. It should be called community development,' she said. Nodding in agreement, I knew I'd found the right guidance and support to embark on this growth journey. Tired of feeling aimless, I acknowledged I required support at this point.

Over the coming months, I immersed myself in the program, embracing the guidance of world-class speakers and coaches from across the globe. Despite the challenges posed by COVID restrictions, it provided me with the solitude necessary to do the work. The isolation heightened feelings of loneliness, however I also saw this as an opportunity to focus on my personal growth. With John's schedule shifting to longer absences due to the pandemic, it provided a focus, distracting me from the aloneness.

The workshops overflowed with new knowledge, tools and strategies, demanding unwavering accountability on every call. Taking action became non-negotiable, pushing me to confront deeply ingrained fears through vulnerable coaching sessions. Despite unyielding efforts to improve my quality of life, I came to realise that my lack of progress stemmed not from a lack of effort, but from being entangled in limiting beliefs. They were keeping me trapped in a cycle of people pleasing, fearful of fully expressing my emotions. The desperate effort to avoid impacting others was preventing me from moving through my own grief process.

In-between sessions, I transformed one of our rooms into a yoga and meditation area adding all the elements you would hope to see in an inviting relaxation space. On the wall I placed the vision board a friend had helped me create together with a beautiful framed quote printed on parchment paper another friend had gifted me. Her gift had reduced me to tears when I had read it. 'I thought of you straight away when I saw it,' she shared through a warm embrace.

The words, *May you trust that you are exactly where you are meant to be,* my daily reminder to stay present. I have read that quote every morning since and the words sustained me through many dark days. The words, *May you be content with yourself just the way you are,* remind me to embrace the new me despite the changes. I could no longer prioritise whether others accepted this changed version of myself. It was my own acceptance that mattered most.

One of the coaches who worked with us introduced us to the concept of having an inner sheep and inner lion. He explained that our sheep is our head, our ego, the version of us that holds us back, filling us with fear, excuses and self-doubt. 'Your sheep can only exist in the future or the past, so if you are always thinking about the past or future, then your sheep is constantly running the show,' he explained.

He encouraged us to start building self-awareness around our thoughts and explained that the simple answer to letting thoughts go is to take action in the opposite direction. Instead of spending time thinking and talking, escape that by taking action. 'The moment you take action, it changes the feeling, and that changes everything.'

Faced with roadblock after roadblock, my energy to continue taking action had dwindled. I had always been an action taker.

However, finding myself in circumstances where multiple limitations were preventing action, I felt stuck. In this stagnation, I had lost confidence, yet I desperately wanted change. I knew I was stuck in my head with unhelpful thoughts and with so many setbacks, nothing was changing them. *If action was the answer, what action could I take?* I questioned with frustration. *I can't even wash my own hair anymore. I can't mop the floor. I can't bend down to do gardening. Supermarkets are so cold I can't even enter them. My eye is so dry and sore I can't read a book anymore. My once sharp mind feels scrambled. My memory is failing. Driving is frightening. I'm constantly exhausted, physically and mentally. Eating is so difficult. Then there's the pain …* The list was endless. I felt like a failure.

What followed next would be my turning point. During the session, I courageously shared, 'At the moment I feel like I've lost confidence in taking action. I feel like I need to regain confidence first.'

Immediately he began coaching me through my thoughts as the group watched on, listening as I leant in, desperate for change. 'We have it around the wrong way. We think we need to *feel* something before we take action but it doesn't work like that. If we take action, *then* we feel confident. The feeling comes *after* the doing. What are you confident in?' he asked

'Feels like nothing anymore,' I replied despondently.

'Stop. Your sheep is talking. We all let it speak. It's a master manipulator and will talk you into believing whatever it wants,' he explained. 'This is where self-awareness is incredibly important. You have to be able to see what you said is not true. You have to see when your sheep is speaking. You have to shut it up because it wants to be heard, it wants to justify what you are thinking. What are you confident in?' he asked again.

Struggling to speak, I searched for answers while he waited. 'Supporting friends and family when I can,' I replied, pausing before adding, 'Aspects of photography, maybe.'

Heidi interjected, explaining my circumstances to the group before asking, 'Denise, when you do take small steps, can you pause and acknowledge yourself for doing it?' Feeling the build-up of shame for the little I could now do and the unease that came with acknowledging myself in front of others, I felt my eyes brimming with tears as she continued. 'For you to have energy to support anyone else, it's incredible. When you do it, you need to acknowledge yourself for doing it. Stop and say, I did this today. Be proud of yourself for every baby step. It's not your usual bar, which is way up high, but it's progress. If you do small steps all the time, the shift is massive.'

An inability to acknowledge the small things I achieved had been an issue the entire time. My journalling had helped somewhat, but recently, very little I did felt worthy of mention. I felt like a failure in so many areas. My life had shrunk. I had shrunk. I felt of little use to anyone, including myself.

'Go pick up your camera and take some photos and you will feel confident because you create the emotion from your action. If you do things that make you feel confident, you will feel confident,' he said. 'You were born confident. There is no such thing as an insecure baby. Insecurity is what you were taught. You *learnt* how to be insecure.' He reminded us our sheep is obsessed with perfection, but our lion only cares about progress.

When asked if I would consider myself an overthinker, I laughed, 'Yes. Definitely.'

'Your sheep uses overthinking, its go-to tool, to beat the crap out of you. Why do you ask so many questions?' he asked.

Pausing in reflection, I replied, 'To understand myself I guess.'

'What's that going to do for you?' he asked.

A surge of vulnerability swept through me. 'I guess I'm trying to work out why I'm feeling the way I am. Maybe because I berate myself about things I should've done better in the past. I'm always thinking about what I could've done differently or better,' I replied.

'This is the overthinking. We all struggle with these things. They are just expressed in different ways. What are you getting out of understanding?' he asked.

As I searched for answers, I sensed deep emotions brewing. 'Maybe trying to explain myself,' I replied.

'You can keep asking questions but it's creating suffering. What would happen if you stopped thinking about the past and the future?' he asked.

'Peace. I'd have peace,' I replied as I exhaled.

'It's your choice,' he said. 'You are sacrificing peace if you keep analysing and asking questions. Our memories are flawed because they have the influence of our own perspective and belief system, but we dig into them.' Frustrated my thoughts remained so ingrained, I felt rising desperation for long-term change.

'What's the benefit you get from overthinking?' he asked.

My mind was blank. If it wasn't understanding, what was it? 'I don't know,' I repeated.

'You do. That's the sheep trying to stop you. How does overthinking hold you back in life?' he asked.

The answer was in this question. 'It's holding me back from happiness. And acceptance,' I admitted.

'Do you not believe you deserve happiness and acceptance?' he enquired.

'I want it, but ...' I paused. 'Maybe I've connected it with worthiness.'

'Why are you punishing yourself? Don't think about it just say it,' he asked.

Unable to contain my emotions, hot tears streamed down my cheeks. 'I've been punished all my life,' I blurted out. 'All I hear is what I do wrong.'

'So, what is the belief you have about yourself?' he asked.

'I'm not worthy. I'm not deserving. I'm not okay as I am. I'm a bad person because nothing I do is good enough,' I shared, unable to hide my sadness as tears fell.

'You are punishing yourself. When you say, "I'm not worthy, I'm not deserving," is that your truth or is it your perspective?' he asked.

Sharing with honesty, I replied, 'I *feel* like it's the truth.'

'I don't care, is it the truth?' he probed further.

As I sat with his question, I replied what I knew but did not feel, 'No it's not the truth.'

Saddened by my own beliefs, I listened carefully as he explained, 'You were conditioned to believe it. And then at some point you accepted it as the truth. Here's the truth. At some point you wore that sheep mask long enough that you finally decided, I'm a sheep. You've been told you're not good enough, you're this, you're that, for so long that you finally at some point said, that's who I am, and it became your identity. And you've been punishing yourself ever since.'

Allowing myself to feel the emotions his words evoked, I recognised how damaging my thoughts were. Regardless of my efforts, even my inability to shift them felt like failure. His words were undoubtably an accurate representation of my reality.

'What you must realise is, it's only a perspective. You think thoughts that punish you,' he explained.

A lifetime of external voices had been punishing me and I had believed them, taking these voices on myself. Recalling past words from Heidi, 'You're oblivious to the obstacle you've become to yourself,' I felt the full weight of responsibility to change my belief systems. *To what? If I wasn't what I'd believed all my life, then who was I?*

'You believe you are the sheep when in reality you are the lion. The only problem you have is you don't know who the hell you are. That's the only problem any human being on this planet has,' he shared. Confronted with the words, 'You don't know who you are,' I could see how far my thoughts had dragged me down again. I had slipped back into old habits.

'If you realised who you truly are, the person you were born to be, the incredible loving soul you are, you wouldn't punish yourself. All you have to do is remember who you are and act in alignment with this person. Then the negative thinking, the negative emotions will disappear,' he explained.

Silently, I nodded in understanding when asked, 'What would happen if you loved yourself as much as you loved everyone else? Would you punish that person you love? You punish yourself because you believe you're *not* that person. You falsely punish yourself because you are not who you believe you really are. You just have to focus on who you are, Denise.'

At that point I felt an overwhelming sadness at the pain I had caused myself for so many years, believing I wasn't deserving of love. 'Write this question down,' he said. 'What would my greatest self do? That will be the most important question you will ask yourself for the rest of your life. You know the answer. It's an inner knowing.

You don't have to think about it. The thing is you are going to have to go do it and it's going to take courage. But every time you take action in alignment with your greatest self, you get more confidence.'

Feeling a lightness I had not felt for many months, I exhaled, knowing the importance of this work and the courage it would require to create permanent change. My beliefs were stopping me from being me. They needed changing.

When asked by another participant about the value of going back to the past to help us find answers, he explained that the past is merely a tool to gain wisdom. 'Where it gets dangerous is when you live in the past as if it's the current reality. Look back to find what you were supposed to learn from it and apply that wisdom to your current life,' he explained. 'Your past is your personal Google. Get your answer then close it and move forward with your life.'

That evening after the session, I opened my journal and recorded at the top of my page, *So, who the hell am I?* Flicking through my journal, I read through my notes from a masterclass with another coach on knowing and actioning our values. 'Your values are your worth so if you don't know them, you don't know your worth. If you feel out of alignment, ask if you know your values and are you practising them.'

Reflecting on my notes, I recognised my people pleasing often led me away from living my values as I pushed my own needs aside to meet the needs of others.

'If you are a people pleaser, if you are constantly bending over backwards for people, then you are betraying yourself,' he had shared. 'It's the worst type of betrayal you can have. Once you know your values, you know when to say no. We have limited time on this earth. Every time you say yes to somebody else you are saying no to yourself.'

I knew it was time to confront the barriers to putting my own needs first. My belief that this was selfish felt like an immovable block. It was a belief that needed changing.

'If it doesn't feel right in your gut, this is where you can start putting yourself first and say no. People will get upset with you in the beginning but if you don't, you'll be the one who ends up suffering. If everyone on this planet understood their values and worth, they wouldn't put their stuff on other people and they'd all start to accept each other as they are.'

People will get upset with you. Those words unsettled me, but where was people pleasing getting me? Regardless of how hard I tried, I still wasn't enough. A flaw would be found, a criticism shared, and I would work harder to please, subconsciously ignoring my own needs to avoid displeasing anyone. If I had done all I could and more, and still I was judged, my only strategy left was to withdraw to avoid further pain.

I would learn later that this withdrawal created the fear I avoided, only it was me creating the abandonment. While obvious in hindsight, my childhood survival strategy of withdrawing or over-giving, was rooted in a deep fear of rejection. Avoiding criticism was a way to feel safe and protected. It was automatic. It had been a successful survival strategy as a child, under the illusion of being protective.

Now, despite my efforts to fight for my life, fear of criticism had seen my withdrawal strategy kick into full swing. Trying everything to find a way to lessen the impact on others, yet failing, I had believed it was in my best interest to put on my best smile when I could, and withdraw when I couldn't.

As I reached the three-month stage in the program, we were challenged to share the action we had taken on our purpose plan within 48 hours. I had initially signed up for the program from a place of survival. Amidst a battle for my life, I hadn't anticipated I would be making any major life-changing decisions. Despite this, through the program I had discovered options that were potentially manageable providing my situation improved. My desire to find ways to bring joy into my days had not waned.

At times, I wondered, had I just not accepted my circumstances or was it simply a desperate search for a reason to live? Was I holding on to hope my condition would improve and good days were coming? Or was it because others didn't believe or accept my situation? Was I avoiding the shame of their perceptions by trying to convince myself I could find that elusive solution? Maybe I would be seen as a failure if I couldn't get on and do something with my life. Maybe it was all of this.

Even though the nagging thought I was dreaming of impossibilities hovered, I continued with the task of defining a clear purpose and outlining steps to propel me towards my goals. We had been coached to cultivate unwavering certainty in our purpose. My purpose was centred around ways I could contribute to the lives of others in a meaningful way. It was a missing element I had long sought to integrate back into my life. Shame had continued to bite at my heels each day I was unable to work.

Over the course of my program, I had explored life coaching as it provided the flexibility necessary to accommodate my ongoing health challenges. It would enable me to do as little or as much as I could handle, even if it was once a month. Although I longed to return to teaching, I had finally come to terms with the fact it was unquestionably out of my reach.

Taking a leap of faith, I promptly enrolled in a three-day online seminar with The Coaching Institute, a Melbourne-based life coaching company. After the second day of the seminar, I decided it was a good choice. Once they granted me special permission to extend the time I completed the course, I committed to pursuing a life coaching qualification. Finally, I had a concrete plan for a more meaningful existence. Regardless of the outcome, human behaviour was an area of interest I knew I would enjoy. I held no expectations about using the qualification if it proved too much. With no time pressure, and learning accessible via webinars, video and audio content, there were fewer hurdles to overcome.

Working with Heidi two years earlier, she had planted a seed about writing and publishing my story. 'Your story needs telling,' she urged. I knew she was right but back then, the timing wasn't. Her suggestion recently resurfaced, reigniting my interest. Overwhelmed at the magnitude of such a project, I researched various options. Fuelled by the momentum of my purpose plan and the desire to help others by sharing my story, I enrolled in a half-day workshop with Natasa Denman, founder of Ultimate 48-Hour Author. With the appeal of her infectious energy, coupled with the option to work independently through her online course content at my own pace, I signed up to her program.

Sharing my ambitious commitments within the timeframe, still in disbelief, Heidi laughed, shaking her head as she replied, 'You signed up for both? Of course you did. You need to choose one, not both.'

Her laughter echoed my all-or-nothing approach, exposing my tendency to overcommit. Despite the progress made over the past few months, it was clear more work lay ahead. While my energy and mood had lifted with new clarity, I needed to remain cautious. My pain persisted, and fatigue remained a constant companion. The intensity of the Illuminate program had already drained me. Natasa's workshop had solidified my desire to write my book, but Heidi's wisdom struck a chord. The book would have to wait. In the meantime, I resolved to voice record any material as ideas emerged, knowing the project could wait a year or two.

In our final session, given the chance to provide feedback, I spoke from my heart about the life-saving impact of their program. 'Back in April, I was in a dark place,' I began, the memories still fresh. 'I confided in my husband and a friend that I felt no reason to live. I didn't think I could go on. Living with my condition felt unbearable. But after the first session, I knew I'd be okay. While John went fishing, I threw myself into the program, determined to work on myself. I knew I had to.'

Reflecting on a pivotal moment, I continued, 'When you gave us 48 hours to make a decision on our plans,' I hesitated, struggling to contain my emotions, 'I realised I hadn't joined the program to make a decision; I had joined just to work out how to stay alive. But I said to myself, "F*ck it, I'm going to do it." That's when I signed up to study life coaching and committed to writing my book about my experience, hoping to help others.' Emotion welled up as I continued, 'Your program has been profoundly impactful. I'm here today because of you. Without it, I don't think I would have made it to June or July.'

Tears streamed down my face as I acknowledged my transformation. 'I know I'll face challenges but I'm leaving with a deeper understanding of myself and a renewed sense of purpose,' I admitted, my voice trembling. 'It's not the same one I had five years ago, pre-shingles, but I'm determined to find reasons to stay on this earth, no matter how tough it gets. Thank you, from the bottom of my heart, and from my family as well.'

There was a poignant silence before I glanced at my screen. I was met with a sea of emotional faces peering back at me. I scanned the screen for Heidi's face as she began to speak. 'For those who may not know Denise, when she mentions she's living with chronic pain, it is so beyond that. For her to even sit up, get up and join us on every call is amazing. For those grappling with excuses, there's always someone who gives you perspective.'

Her words were like a warm embrace, validating my experience in ways I couldn't fully express. 'I just high five you, Denise,' she continued, her admiration evident. 'Every time we get to work together my mouth is always hanging open with what your capabilities are. Every single time, you reach new levels. I feel grateful to be able to work with you again.'

Her encouragement, validation and understanding ignited a profound sense of gratitude. 'Thank you.' I managed, tears quietly streaming down my face. 'I'll be forever grateful,' I replied, though the words felt inadequate for the depth of emotion they carried.

28.

LIFE COACHING

*'People will do more to avoid pain than
they will do to gain pleasure.'*
Tony Robbins

Embarking on my life coaching studies in August 2020, I immersed myself in a new world of learning. Thanks to COVID, studying from home became a viable option, perfect for my circumstances. The three-day introduction, Foundations of Coaching Success, marked the beginning of my journey. From the first session, the presenter's engaging and personable approach had me captivated.

I immediately found the content interesting and witnessed the fascination of coaching in action. Surprised by the depth of information presented over those three days, I initially worried about my ability to retain anything. However, the collaborative learning approach through online break-out rooms created the ideal learning environment.

After completing the introduction, my 18-month learning process began. Weekly webinars delved into the intricacies of human behaviour, while hands-on coaching sessions provided invaluable practical experience. It required six hours of flexible study time each week. The transformational nature of the coaching process was astounding and I felt privileged to witness clients making new discoveries and connections. It also opened a window into the trauma experienced by many, revealing its impact on beliefs and behaviours.

Managing my expectations became crucial as I navigated through the course. For me, it meant lowering the bar of what I expected from myself. Fatigue emerged as a significant challenge, particularly as I began my coaching hours. Each session left me exhausted for the next two days. Despite this, I persisted, pacing myself meticulously. I allowed myself breaks or weeks off whenever it was necessary. Though COVID restrictions deepened the sense of disconnection, coaching helped alleviate the devastating impact of added isolation.

With purpose infused into my days and my mind engaged in learning, a glimmer of hope for a brighter future began to emerge. However, balancing coaching studies with the impact of chronic pain proved to be an exhaustive and daunting task. Three months into the program, weariness had intensified. Amidst my already loaded regime of medical appointments, new dental issues stemming from my condition also added to the complexity. The pressure of clenching through pain was causing abfractions, loss of tooth structure. Multiple dental repairs became necessary, along with fitting a custom mouthguard to safeguard my teeth. Reassuring myself that this additional fatigue was temporary, I requested another extension to my studies to allow for an even slower pace.

By the end of the fourth month, my exhaustion reached its peak. With six friends coming to the river for a night to celebrate John's birthday, I gave myself a week off to rest beforehand. Despite my overwhelming fatigue, the evening was enjoyable. However, my joy was short-lived. The following day, a deep burning pain had developed in my left shoulder. Concerned, I asked John to check. Looking closely, he said, 'There's three red dots in a row. It's really red.'

Exhaling in disbelief, I said, 'It's shingles again. I can't believe this. I should have recognised it coming. I felt more weary than usual last week and on the weekend my legs felt almost unresponsive every time I went upstairs to bring food down. I should know by now.' Frustrated and disappointed, I returned my gaze to the screen. While I knew the toll coaching was taking on me, I did not want to accept it. Choking back tears, I refused to entertain the idea of giving up my studies. It was a source of fulfilment and purpose in my life, and I was determined to persevere. Walking downstairs, I retrieved the box of antiviral medications, grateful I had been advised to always keep them on hand. *Damn this body of mine.*

Taking a break from my studies for three weeks, I focused on resting before reducing my coaching hours to one per week. 100 coaching hours were required to become a credentialed life coach and I needed to build my hours up in preparation for assessment with my mentor. For my nine assessment sessions, my designated client was another student, who would later become a wonderful friend. Before my first assessment, we met over Zoom to become acquainted and immediately connected. During our discussions, I discovered she was an experienced coach herself. Throughout our studies, she became a wonderful mentor and guide.

At the completion of one of my assessment sessions, the coaching mentor shared my strengths. As she had finished, I immediately asked if she had any suggestions for areas I needed to improve.

'Did you hear my feedback?' she asked.

'Yes, but I would love some feedback on what areas I can work on?' I asked again.

'It was an amazing session. You need to take that on board. All you need to do is keep practising and building your hours up,' she said, frowning at me.

Frustrated with what I saw as a lack of feedback, I spoke to the student I coached after the session. She noticed I hadn't really taken in what my assessor stated I had done well and had only sought information about what to practise and improve. Finding positive feedback both unreliable and uncomfortable to receive, I always waited for words telling me what I needed to do better. There was always something to improve on.

Slowly accumulating coaching hours, I found great fulfilment in guiding others through their healing. It was a privilege to be entrusted with their vulnerabilities and to witness their transformation. However, the toll it continued to take on my energy was undeniable. Fatigue, coupled with increased pain and disrupted sleep, signalled a message I couldn't yet face. Within months, shingles struck again – a stark reminder my body was desperately trying to communicate I was pushing it beyond its limits. I knew I was facing another failed attempt in my pursuit to find fulfilment.

Regardless of my determination to make coaching work, I couldn't ignore the impact on my health, nor that I was still giving my energy to others at the expense of my own wellbeing. Recognising this pattern, and knowing two further episodes of shingles was more than enough warning, I made the difficult decision to step back from coaching. Was it admitting defeat or was it acceptance? Perhaps both.

Having completed the course material, I focused on slowly taking my time and fulfilling my final coaching hours, knowing life coaching would end there. The desire to coach lingered for many months, however my health told me otherwise. Despite a tempting offer of employment as a life coach, I knew it was time to prioritise my own healing. I had been given all the skills and tools I needed yet kept hearing, and feeling, that something was blocking my progress. I knew I had only skimmed the surface. I wanted to confront my own trauma head on and address the roots of deep-seated beliefs behind my pattern of over-giving.

The wealth of knowledge I gained opened my eyes to the layers of healing yet to be uncovered. It also showed me the power of healing. I began recognising patterns and beliefs stemming from my own traumatic experiences and sensed their lingering effects. Triggers served as reminders of unhealed wounds waiting to be addressed. Fear had prevented me from diving into trauma therapy, however it was something I couldn't postpone any longer.

I had been recommended a skilled trauma therapist specialising in EMDR therapy, therapy designed to alleviate the intensity of traumatic memories. Accepting I even carried trauma was a daunting realisation, one that took time to fully digest.

Deciding to prioritise my own self-care and healing over perceived or real external pressures to 'get on with life' and 'move on from my chronic pain condition' was a significant shift. Surrendering the endless striving to get well, or appear well, brought about an unexpected sense of calm. Giving up the tireless attempts to keep trying, keep striving, had previously felt like defeat rather than an act of self-care and self-compassion. *Could I give myself permission to focus on my own healing? Would it be seen as weak, or even selfish? Was I ready?* I would soon come to realise that facing trauma was far from weak. Ultimately, it was a confronting, painful and selfless choice. It required a quiet, relentless kind of strength, one built on courage, perseverance and a deep will to heal.

While I waited for my first appointment with the trauma therapist in the latter half of 2021, I decided to find a small volunteer role as a way to contribute and find purpose. Inspired by my experience coaching individuals impacted by trauma, I explored volunteering in the mental health field and decided to pursue training Gracie as a therapy dog. Her senses were incredibly attuned to me on difficult days. She would lie on me, her chin resting on mine, staring right through me like she could see into my soul. She never left my side during some of my most fearful moments, gently pawing me as the agony ripped through my face. With her perfect temperament, she was an ideal candidate, allowing me to contribute in an area I felt passionate about. Having experienced the stigma of mental health first-hand, I also felt called to play my part in creating positive change, no matter how small.

After completing the required training and assessment, I was granted a placement in the mental health ward of a public hospital. Despite our visits lasting only an hour, the impact Gracie had on both staff and patients was remarkable. I recall one psychiatrist pulling me aside, emphasising, 'Don't ever underestimate the difference you make. It's much calmer after your visit.' Each visit was filled with soul-filling moments, offering rewards that outweighed any exhaustion experienced afterward. Gracie had changed my own life and I loved to see others experience the difference she could make.

While my volunteer role couldn't replace the impact of life coaching, I started noticing changes in myself brought about by my coaching journey. The lessons I learnt naturally seeped into my interactions and changed the way I communicated with others. Understanding human behaviours and reactions deepened my compassion even further. My responses in conversations were more meaningful and supportive and friends and family even began acknowledging the positive changes they noticed in me. It hadn't been for nothing. It was a wonderful skill and knowledge base to draw on through life.

Therapy dog team

29.

RELIEF

'When we are no longer able to change a situation, we are challenged to change ourselves.'
Viktor Frankl

With the dream of life coaching behind me, I was forced to confront the futility of my attempts to return to work. Beneath it all, I recognised how many of those efforts had often been driven not just by my own needs but by outside pressure, both real and perceived. The endless suggestions, 'Why don't you do this? Why don't you do that? What are you going to do?' chipped away at me. Finally, I understood it was time to change course. No more 'should', no more 'have to'. It was time to reclaim my life and step into the role of director of my own story.

I began addressing neglected areas of my life that had long been overshadowed by my desperate pursuit of purpose and pain relief. This marked the beginning of a rebuilding phase, where I sought to carefully and steadily improve various aspects of my life: contribution, personal growth, nutrition, fun and recreation, social connections and hobbies.

Volunteering and pursuing my own studies in trauma education offered small but meaningful ways to address the life areas of contribution and personal growth. Acknowledging the importance of maintaining my health, especially given my lowered immunity from multiple bouts of shingles, I wanted to turn my attention to my nutritional intake. Managing my pain would require setting boundaries to protect my energy, a self-care strategy I had long struggled to implement. It wouldn't be until I began EMDR that I truly understood how much energy healing demanded, and how essential periods of solace would be. I finally heeded the advice my GP had suggested from the beginning, 'You need to focus on your own daily living before you can give to others,' a message echoed by my entire medical team, and by John. I had to admit that managing chronic pain consumed much of my energy and demanded acceptance and adaptation. No longer swimming against the tide, I aimed to find fulfilling moments with trusted loved ones when opportunities arose. It was time to prioritise self-care and genuine connection.

In July 2021, I discovered the possibility of legally accessing medicinal marijuana, cannabidiol (CBD), to manage my pain. With so many failed attempts at relief, I was naturally sceptical about its effectiveness in easing nerve pain. Encouragement from my daughter and therapists prompted me to consider it as a potential solution. Managing my pain remained a continuous battle of the mind, still too often leaving me wishing for an end just to bring respite. With some hesitation, I discussed the option with my GP, who wholeheartedly supported the idea. With her encouragement, I booked an appointment with an integrative doctor able to prescribe it.

As I sat in yet another waiting room, I pondered what the process would entail. To my surprise, after a thorough assessment of my condition, I walked out 30 minutes later with a bottle in hand.

That night marked the beginning of my journey with CBD. The process required a gradual approach, slowly building up the dosage over time. Despite the putrid taste and stomach discomfort, I persevered week after week, incrementally increasing my dose in anticipation of miraculous relief. For months, I battled the relentless side effects of fatigue, headaches, nausea and dizziness. Determined, I persevered, encouraged by the doctor to take it slow and space each increase two to four weeks apart. Based on experiences with other patients, he felt confident it would provide relief, but I had learnt to carry no expectations.

As part of my treatment, he also suggested regular intravenous vitamin supplementation. He emphasised the importance of scrutinising my diet, particularly eliminating sugar. Understanding the detrimental effects of sugar on my pain, I knew I couldn't ignore his advice. Sugar had re-entered my diet, a battle I had previously conquered for almost four years until emotional eating resurfaced a year ago through my struggle with aloneness. Gradually, it had morphed into an uncontrollable sugar addiction. During times of emotional distress, consuming chocolate was my default coping mechanism.

With a referral to a dietician in November, I embarked on an 18-month process to overhaul my approach to eating. Navigating the intricacies of my diet with the dietician was an exhaustive yet enlightening journey. We explored every aspect, from the challenges of chewing and its impact on my pain levels, to overall nutrition and emotional eating. In the past year I had introduced soft chewable food, yet there were times when the pain was so intense eating became unbearable. As a result, my food intake fluctuated, impacting my overall nutrition and immunity. Unable to tolerate chewing on my left side, I had adapted to a new way of eating, shifting from a lifetime habit of chewing predominantly on the left side to the right. Even this adjustment brought its own set of questions in respect to pain and fatigue in my jaw. *Should I continue with cautious chewing on one side or attempt to distribute it evenly? Would smaller, more frequent meals be better than larger ones?* The complexities seemed endless.

With the guidance of the oral and maxillofacial surgeon, and the dietician's expertise, we devised a plan tailored to my needs. While there were no easy answers, grazing wasn't recommended. Sticking with softer foods was encouraged, and sitting down to a steak probably wasn't an achievable goal.

'The repetitive nature of having to be cautious and conscious of your food takes a lot of mental energy. We want to make it as simple as we can,' the dietician shared. My current process carried a significant mental load, each meal a calculated endeavour to manage pain and ensure proper nutrition.

The dietician meticulously addressed every facet of my diet, including identifying self-sabotaging behaviours linked to emotional eating. She recognised my tendency toward an all-or-nothing approach through strict dietary restrictions over almost four years. She also identified that eating food I knew would make my pain worse reflected deeper issues of self-worth and a rebellion against such tight constraints in my diet. The exploration continued to reveal surprises, highlighting the habits I needed to break along the way.

Discovering that my sugar cravings were more than just a habit was a significant revelation. They were, in fact, an addiction, reflecting an underlying unmet need. 'An emotional relationship with food can stem a long way back with people. In early childhood, not in your teens. When something has an emotional attachment to it, we remember it more,' the dietician had shared. 'No wonder it takes so long to overcome.'

This realisation brought clarity to a lifelong struggle that had often been dismissed as simply having a *sweet tooth*. Memories from my childhood, like my sneaky attempts to grab extra sweets, underscored the depth of my relationship with sugar. I often secretly snuck into the pantry, diving into the Milo tin with a dessertspoon when no-one was around, quickly filling my mouth and disappearing before I was discovered. I even tried a spoonful of Sunshine powdered milk one day, just for some sweetness, only to find it stuck in the roof of my mouth like glue. Sometimes, I scooped out a teaspoon of jam or snuck into the freezer for a spoon of ice-cream. Chocolates were a rarity, although my mother often had her own stash in the house, hidden in suitcases within suitcases, that we were not to touch.

I shared with the dietician I had recently caught up with my aunty, who told stories of my antics around cakes or biscuits. The conversation had sparked laughter and nostalgia, highlighting the enduring nature of this aspect of my personality. Laughing, I had asked her, 'What age did you notice I started looking for sweet food?' I had recently had my first session with the trauma therapist and, combined with all I had uncovered through kinesiology, I was curious to check the age connection.

'Around seven I think,' she replied.

Bingo! In kinesiology sessions, age seven frequently surfaced, intertwined with almost every trapped emotion we explored. I have the most vivid recollections of my time in distress when alone in hospital at this age. My grandmother once visited briefly during that time, leaving me a bag of lollies. It was the only visit I received during my two weeks in hospital. I stared in disbelief at the lollies. I'd never had access to a whole bag in my entire life. Watching her depart after what felt like barely two minutes, my body trembled in fear, believing I would die from aloneness. The intensity of the fear consumed every moment of my period of hospitalisation. At night, it escalated to the point I would wet myself out of sheer terror. I lay awake in the darkness most nights, desperate for my parents' return, until the weight of disappointment each morning crushed any hope of their arrival. In the absence of their nurture, the distress from the unbearable sensations coursing through my body was so overwhelming I could barely breathe.

At each subsequent hospital visit, I gradually grew attached to one of the nurses. She allowed me to accompany her on her rounds as I recovered. She didn't speak much but had a gentle soul and a warm, beautiful smile. Somehow, she always seemed to appear at my bedside when I felt most vulnerable, as if guided by an inner knowing. In my later years of hospitalisation, I discovered that she had often visited me even on her days off, always wearing her familiar blue knitted cardigan. She would never know the comfort and relief I felt whenever I caught a glimpse of that cardigan in my doorway. I trailed after her on her rounds like a loyal companion, my eyes fixated on her every move. Perhaps she found it an easier way to accommodate my frequent use of the buzzer. I would fabricate any excuse for someone to come and alleviate my silent, yet intense, internal distress. If she wasn't on duty, often no-one came, or they took so long my distress escalated further. Perhaps they had figured out my tactic. Maybe I *didn't* need eight jugs of water in one day. Despite my anguish, I complied with instructions and refrained from crying. Inside, I longed to scream for my mother, to plead, 'I'm so scared, please don't leave me alone.' I couldn't fathom why I had been abandoned. With nothing to occupy my time, often tethered to oxygen and intravenous drips, my emotions intensified as I lay there. I would reach into my drawer and indulge in a lolly to ease the distress. The sugar provided the comfort I yearned for in my parents' absence. Each day, when the emotional weight became too much to bear, instead of crying out or pleading for company, I would open the drawer next to my bed and take another lolly.

'Going for chocolate is you wanting to feel comforted,' the dietician shared. 'Recognise this as the little girl in you seeking that comfort. Our habits are deeply ingrained, and the connection remains. You're trying to break a habit that brings you temporary comfort. You need to cultivate new habits to replace the old ones.'

Living with chronic pain was isolating, especially during the long stretches alone at home. It was no surprise I slipped back into old habits that promised instant relief, even if fleeting and followed by self-reproach. Besides, the sugar only exacerbated my pain, fuelling it like stoking a fire with petrol. The core issue had to be addressed. What I truly needed was companionship. I had to persist in seeking out feasible opportunities to connect with others. I needed to find alternative ways to fulfil my need for comfort. Understanding the root of my self-sabotage shed light on my next steps.

'Not working, it feels empty. It's not the norm and you are the minority. Finding fulfilment within yourself is important and a lot of people struggle with this,' she explained. 'People judging you also prevents you from reaching out to connect. Surround yourself with people you trust and work on being comfortable in your own company. Discover activities you enjoy doing alone.'

The dietician's willingness to collaborate with my other specialists, and her comprehensive analysis of my entire situation provided me with the necessary tools to understand how to support myself holistically. Her insight into my self-sabotaging behaviours prompted me to work with the trauma therapist to address childhood wounds being triggered by my current circumstances of being alone so much. Each day at home was like ongoing exposure therapy. It subconsciously took me back to recurrent lengthy periods left on my own, sick and in pain, throughout my childhood.

With life coaching no longer occupying my schedule, I sought nearby social activities I could manage. Thankfully, another timely opportunity presented itself. A friend introduced me to Wednesday morning social table tennis, and I eagerly accepted her invitation despite fears of losing my balance.

Table tennis soon became a cherished highlight of my week. Regardless of the weather, it provided an accessible and joyful social activity. On my first day, in early November 2021, I quickly discovered the need to be cautious whenever I bent to pick up the ball. In my first game, I noticed the changes to my peripheral vision and the delayed eye tracking saw balls go by I couldn't see. The ever-present feeling of floating intensified with faster head movements, leaving me feeling like I'd just returned from a month at sea. I questioned whether I had pushed myself too far too soon.

Despite these challenges, I found humour in the situation, often likening the experience to playing under the influence. I adapted by incorporating pauses between hits and adjusting my head movements accordingly. The camaraderie among the players, a kind, lively and joyful group of women, infused the room with laughter throughout the entire morning.

Engaging in table tennis brought much-needed enjoyment and social interaction into my week, yet it also came with setbacks. Returning home for lunch on Wednesdays, I always noticed an increase in the swelling around my eye and face, accompanied by my nerves throwing a raucous dance party. My tongue was more swollen than usual (possibly from all the chatter), my ear thumped, and my lower lip and chin struggled to coordinate drinking from a cup unless I used a straw. The aftermath of me having fun. Despite these frustrating setbacks, I refused to let them dampen my spirits or hinder my social engagement. Experiences of joy was my focus.

To mitigate the effects, every second Wednesday afternoon I began scheduling appointments with a myofascial and craniosacral therapist. The treatment relieved pain by both soothing the nerves and reducing inflammation and tightness. Attending Yin yoga every Wednesday evening provided further relief for my agitated nerves. While enjoying table tennis came with significant consequences, the positive impact on my mental wellbeing made the effort worthwhile.

During this period, I ventured into attending occasional free two-hour photography workshops run by Canon. At one workshop held at the zoo, I met a photographer who encouraged me to join her local camera club. Despite having lost confidence in reaching out, I embraced the invitation and soon developed a wonderful connection with her and others through our shared love of photography. It not only provided an opportunity to fill the need for connection, but the immersive nature of photography also provided a welcome distraction from my pain, making it an ideal hobby.

In addition to these social opportunities, a friend extended the invitation to join her family for dinner once a month during John's absences. I eagerly embraced the chance to spend quality time with them and enjoy their easy, supportive company. Recognising the toll that socialising could take on my pain levels, I learnt to prioritise rest on that day. However, the companionship of cherished friends far outweighed the risk of increased pain. On those occasions, I allowed myself the grace to rest and recuperate fully the following day.

One morning early in December, I noticed a subtle decrease in my pain. It lingered throughout the day. Tentatively optimistic, I kept it to myself, hesitant to raise false hopes. By lunchtime the following day, the change was still evident. *Could this be real?* I wondered, surprised by its consistency over two consecutive days. Though the pain remained, its intensity had noticeably diminished. Seated on the couch, I surveyed our living space, puzzled by the feeling of ease in my body.

Gone were the tense, shallow breaths and the agitation that had haunted me since April 2016. Instead, I found myself able to breathe more slowly and deeply, something I hadn't experienced in over five and a half years. While the burning ache and sharp stabs of pain persisted, they weren't threatening to overwhelm me like a knife-wielding intruder constantly attacking my face. I had been slowly increasing my dose of CBD over the past four months. *Could it finally be helping?* Over the next 10 days, I carefully monitored my pain, noting the same encouraging pattern. *Twelve days. That can't be a coincidence,* I thought to myself, bubbling with excitement.

A quiet confidence settled over me. Finally, I turned to John, a hint of a smile lingering in my eyes. 'John, I don't believe I'm imagining this, but my pain has definitely decreased in intensity over the past two weeks,' I shared, 'I'm sure it's improved by at least 10 percent. I'm frightened to say it, but if it stays like this, I think I can live with it. It's only a slight difference, but it's taken the edge off.' Although voicing these words stirred a fear of false hope, it marked the first tangible sign of possible change.

Over the following two months, my pain continued its gradual improvement, eventually stabilising at around 20 percent overall improvement by late January 2022. Despite peaks during moments of tiredness, overusing facial muscles or encountering external triggers, I couldn't deny the progress. Embracing this reawakened optimism, I felt compelled to share my joy with friends and family who had closely followed my journey. Cautiously, I began communicating the change, knowing many had long hoped for good news but, like me, never truly believed it would come.

Finally, after almost six years of navigating the complexities of my condition, I believed in the possibility I could coexist with my pain with a carefully managed approach. While it wouldn't be without its challenges, it felt attainable. I no longer felt the need to segment my days or merely see each one as a bridge to the next. Despite the persistent presence of chronic pain and fatigue, I embraced the belief I could withstand them. I felt a sudden, overwhelming sense of gratitude for the gift of life.

Murat Bay District Hospital (Ceduna)
My wonderful nurse in her blue cardigan
First hospital stay - age 4 ½

30.

REHABILITATION

'Chronic pain is not all about the body, and it's not all about the brain – it's everything. Target everything. Take back your life.'
Sean Mackey

Despite improvement in my pain, early in 2022, my hearing, balance and dizziness challenges had unfortunately intensified. Quick movements, particularly turning my head, disoriented me and exacerbated my symptoms. Driving necessitated even more caution and I slowed head turns further to allow my vision time to adjust. During walks, stumbling and veering left when I turned my head seemed more prominent.

One morning, I bent to pull out a weed in our garden. Suddenly, I lost my balance and began to fall. Managing to catch myself just in time, I pressed against the house to regain my stability. 'Phew, I'm really dizzy,' I said to John, my vision blurring as I spoke.

'I think you should head in,' John suggested.

'I will,' I agreed, as I bent to remove one last weed. The next thing I remember was waking to find myself laying on the path. John was crouched next to me holding my head, blood covering his hand.

'Why did you lay me here?' I asked, confused.

'I didn't. You fell on your head. I was right behind you, but I couldn't catch you in time,' he replied, his concern evident.

Inevitably, I had no choice but to return to the GP, who referred me to an ENT for further investigation into my hearing and dizziness. Another brain MRI was requested.

Sitting in the waiting room at the ENT appointment, I wondered if I would ever reach a point where this condition stabilised. Its invasive nature knew no bounds. Just when I thought I understood it, something new would arise. After a comprehensive hearing assessment, I was called in to the ENT where he conducted several tests. Combined with the results of the hearing assessment, he revealed the cause of my dizziness and hearing issues.

Finally, after six long years, there were answers. No, I wasn't imagining that voices sounded distant and distorted, as if hearing underwater. Early in my journey, my symptoms had been dismissed by a specialist I saw at the time. Despite confusion, I accepted the assessment. However, today's tests provided a clear diagnosis. There was indeed a hearing loss. The specialist confirmed tinnitus, vertigo, dizziness and the feeling of fullness in my ear, were attributed to a condition called endolymphatic hydrops. This condition resulted from damage to the vestibulocochlear nerve caused by the shingles virus. Another cranial nerve had succumbed to the effects of the virus.

This new discovery brought greater understanding to my symptoms and with it, hope. The ENT shared treatment options aimed at preventing further deterioration of my hearing, and twice daily vestibular exercises were required to assist with the vertigo. Medications were also prescribed to decrease pressure in the inner ear and alleviate the spinning sensation. I was advised to avoid caffeine and alcohol, and switch to a low-sodium diet.

My hearing had progressively deteriorated and I had attributed it to the sensation of fullness and pain I was experiencing. Despite numerous stumbles and falls, including several down our stairs and in the shower, I had remained uncertain of the underlying cause.

Walking out of his room with answers to challenges that had baffled me for the past six years, I felt seen and understood. While I hesitated to allow myself false hope of improvement, I couldn't wait to share my news. *I hadn't been imagining I had hearing and balance issues.*

With a clear understanding of my vestibular issues, we took proactive steps at home, installing a rail running the full length of our stairs. Unfortunately, one of the medications intended to assist with my hearing proved ineffective. Within two weeks of starting it, I began experiencing numbness and tingling in my hands and feet. These symptoms persisted for months and posed significant challenges. Daily incidents of fumbling and dropping items became a common occurrence. Drinking glasses were regular casualties. On my walks, the onset of intense pins and needles made my feet go numb, forcing me to wait for feeling to return before proceeding.

By mid-2022, I began rigorous neurophysiotherapy rehabilitation. I dedicated hours each day to retraining my vestibular system, combining in-person physical therapy sessions with an extensive home program tailored to improve my balance, coordination and gaze stability. During my initial visit, the therapist promptly identified the effects of Ramsay Hunt syndrome. Her concern was palpable when she learnt the duration of my symptoms. 'I don't know how much impact we can have. Seven years is a long time. It's a shame you haven't been here earlier.'

Fighting back tears, I was stunned. I believed I had meticulously covered all bases, yet it seemed there were still stones left unturned. 'I hadn't heard of neurophysiotherapy until my physiotherapist recently brought it up,' I managed to whisper, my voice barely audible.

She promptly referred me to another neurophysiotherapist to begin rehabilitation for the facial palsy caused by the nerve damage. Not only was I unaware that rehabilitation for my facial palsy was possible, I couldn't imagine allowing anyone to touch my face. I would learn that without prompt attention, permanent muscle weakness or hearing loss can be more likely.

Ramsay Hunt syndrome had been mentioned in passing in 2019, but I hadn't given it another thought. The desperate pursuit of pain relief and symptom management had overshadowed much of what I experienced during that period. I was fighting for life each day. Ultimately, Ramsay Hunt syndrome was a complication of the shingles virus. It had affected the facial nerve near my inner ear, leading to facial weakness and paralysis, hearing loss, sensitivity to loud noises, dizziness and tinnitus. The more I learnt, the more I understood how widespread the damage was to so much of my face, head and neck. It was hardly surprising that even basic actions like smiling, laughing, talking, chewing or swallowing proved challenging.

At home, I relentlessly persisted with my rehabilitation program, designed to manage dizziness and imbalance. Even on our camping holidays, I refused to let up. I took my program wherever we went. I stuck my laminated posters to gas hot water services, the back of vehicles and camping laundries. With a laser light strapped around my head, I would stand back, tracing every letter of the alphabet with the laser precisely. I walked back and forth, shaking my head at zebra lines, steadily increasing the challenge as instructed. Nothing would prevent my determination to improve my balance.

Through the neurophysiotherapists, I gained insight into how the damage to the vestibulocochlear nerve was disrupting my central nervous system's ability to process sensory information accurately. My brain struggled to calculate my body's position in relation to my surroundings, significantly impacting my balance. Finally, it made sense why I had difficulty with spatial orientation when I looked left and right to cross the road or when I played table tennis. I could also understand why I veered to my left when I turned my head walking and why I experienced more falls at night. Much later, I would also learn that the unusual fluttering sensation I experienced inside my head after exposure to loud noises was also connected to the nerve damage. Shingles. The gift that keeps on giving.

Two months after beginning the vestibular rehabilitation, I walked into the treatment room for my first session of facial palsy rehabilitation. The neurophysiotherapist greeted me warmly, her cheerful demeanour putting me at ease despite my rising uncertainty about what lay ahead. The idea of someone touching my face felt frightening, yet as she gathered information and conducted her assessment, she effortlessly gained my trust. As she explained the need for therapy, I felt reassured by her explanation of what needed addressing. 'Well, let's try it,' I finally said, a hint of trepidation in my voice. 'Even though it sounds terrifying.' Before taking CBD, the mere thought of anyone touching my face would have sent me running for the hills.

As I lay on the bed, I took a deep breath as she began the treatment. With her fingers inside my mouth and on my face, she gently began stretching and dragging my face from my eye down to my lip and from my ear to my nose. I groaned, tears filling my closed eyes at the pain. 'My goodness, this is tight,' she remarked. Unable to speak, I nodded in agreement. Gradually, the lumps, like rocks, began to soften under her touch. My entire body tensed as I endured the experience, relying on every mindfulness strategy I knew of to cope. When she finally withdrew her hands some 30 minutes later, I commented, 'It doesn't feel good in there.'

'I'm not surprised. It's very bumpy.' After assessing and treating my face, she determined the percent of damage and impact on functionality. It seemed every intricate movement in my face was contributing to the nerve pain. With muscles trying to do the heavy lifting on behalf of the damaged nerves, they were tight and tired. Many had atrophied from lack of use. I began an in-depth exploration into understanding my condition in a way I had never thought possible. She educated me on triggers I had never considered and how to prevent amplification of pain by speaking to it differently. 'You have pain in your face but what your brain does to that pain is it adds an amplification. It's given it a microphone to talk into,' she explained.

Persistent chronic pain was holding my brain and nervous system hostage. Pain was my internal alarm system, and it was behaving like a faulty cuckoo clock, the bird constantly activated and striking at random. It needed retraining. It was stuck in overdrive and supersensitive. She explained that because I was treating my face like a no-go zone, it had become defensive and reactive to normal sensations like standard soft pressure, wind and temperature changes. It required desensitising physically and mentally.

Befriending my pain seemed like the only viable option. Just as I would attempt reconciliation or set boundaries with a friend who hurt me, I learnt to do the same with my pain. When it caused distress, I acknowledged the hurt, but mentally turned my back on it by giving it the cold shoulder when it became particularly vicious. I continued to incorporate distraction techniques like knitting or photography to divert its attention. Often, I'd thank it for reminding me when I needed rest or to pace myself better with words such as, 'Thanks for showing me I've overdone it.' I had been working through similar strategies with my jaw physiotherapist, greeting my pain each morning with kindness. 'Good morning, what shall we do together today?' The pain remained, but with strategies to keep it in check, I hoped to prevent it from having the loudest voice. Though I wanted to scream at it, I spoke to it with kindness. Pain became my ally, guiding me like a personal compass. I learnt to differentiate between messages for my benefit and those causing unnecessary suffering, changing direction accordingly.

Throughout my journey, I had ignored the consistent messages from my pain. My body and mind, fatigued and worn out, craved self-care. Despite the signals, I had pushed through, listening to external voices and old beliefs, disregarding my body's warnings. Pain had been a friendly companion all along. Initially, it halted my relentless over-giving by disrupting my nervous system with a painful, malicious virus. When I ignored this message, the chaos escalated. Like a stubborn mule standing its ground, the pain refused to leave. Roadblocks had constantly appeared, urging me to prioritise my own needs. Ignoring the calls, I persisted, sinking deeper into the quicksand until I realised I had to stop fighting and start listening. I had to work with my pain, not against it. My mind travelled back to the health retreat, six months into my journey, 'Your purpose is simple,' one of the therapists had said, holding my arms at the end of our session. 'It's time to stop. Enough pushing through. You need to go on adventures with John. Nothing more. That's all.'

That's all. No more delusional attempts to work or study. It was time to stop, to just be. So many guiding me had said the same along the way. It was okay to focus on finding fulfilment in the process of living, to make living my purpose and to give it my full attention. It was time to give myself permission to let joy in. It was time to find ways to focus on fun and adventure in a sustainable way.

Together with the neurophysiotherapist, I embarked on reshaping my relationship with pain while I addressed the stiffness in my face. In the initial stages of my shingles attack, I had delved into books on rewiring pain and neuroplasticity, desperate for relief. Despite initially feeling invalidated at the suggestion I could train my brain to manage pain, I pursued the concept regardless. Now having accountability and consistent educational input from the neurophysiotherapist and the jaw physiotherapist, I immersed myself fully in the philosophy.

I began to speak kindly to my pain every day, acknowledging its presence but refusing to let it dictate my life. 'Thanks for reminding me I need to rest,' or 'Yes, I hear you but not now thank you, I've got this.' Instead of blaming myself for self-sabotaging behaviours or fearing environmental triggers, I embraced pain as a companion. Mindfulness and breathing exercises helped me confront it rather than resist it. With the support of positive influences, CBD, mindfulness, yoga, pacing, distraction techniques and dietary adjustments, I found a combination of strategies that offered some relief. Though pain often finished with the last word, these methods together provided enough respite to navigate each day.

The neurophysiotherapist continued to offer invaluable insights to help me refine my pain management strategies. I discovered that my dribbling and difficulty finishing meals stemmed from muscle fatigue and overuse, just like any other muscle in the body. I had to persist and keep using them to build them up. Returning to a liquid diet was forbidden. Working on my book for prolonged sessions always exacerbated pain and my face became droopy, so I needed to carefully pace this work. 'When you're concentrating, you squint more, which contracts the muscles. It's like squatting for hours; it creates rapid facial fatigue,' she explained.

Discussing how to respond when asked about my pain, she emphasised the importance of crafting a new narrative. 'We've been conditioned to give automated responses, but that comes with a psychological toll,' she remarked. 'We might feel sharing an honest narrative about pain is a burden to other people, but it lightens our load by being truthful about how we feel. We are not asking someone to carry the pain for us, or do anything, we are just being truthful about how we feel. If they don't know how to deal with it, that's *their* thing.' Her perspective brought clarity and comfort. Despite the feeling of disconnection it created at times, I had learnt to discern when and where to respond authentically and when to default to automatic responses. Balancing the protection of others' emotions with honesty about my own experiences proved to be a common dilemma shared in pain support groups.

Fatigue had become one of the most challenging elements to my days and I shared this in an appointment one day, 'I feel like I am having a better quality of life on the whole, but I feel more exhausted than I ever have.'

'Exhaustion is not just a pain thing. Are you starting to do more?' she asked.

'Yes, six months ago I couldn't have done what I do now,' I replied. 'I've gradually built things in but the fatigue hits so suddenly, then comes the pain. I feel like I can't quite strike the right balance. My face pain is noticeably worse after socialising and sometimes I feel incapacitated for days afterward.'

'You need to condition yourself. People think that when they have decided to be more productive their body will just snap to it. Because of the journey you have taken, you are not fit for life,' she explained. 'People who come out of a very socially isolating experience and begin re-engaging socially become exhausted quickly. Interacting takes energy. Of course you're tired.'

She encouraged me to take it slowly and continue conditioning myself to the level of fitness social events demand. While I had been told multiple times my pain was permanent and a full recovery is generally not what is seen, I wanted to know I was doing all I could. Always hopeful of hearing a different answer, I asked her one day, 'Do you think I'll improve further or is this it?'

She explained that recovering from something like this is enormously complicated and requires a lot of patience and dedication. 'Many don't have this nor the guidance to persist in pushing forward. Nobody knows your potential. Nobody can say you won't continue to make incremental gains in function and pain control. We have no idea of the limits of your neuroplasticity or how well your cognitive behavioural adaptations will continue to influence the way your pain behaves.'

It was all I needed to hear. My desire to live a better life was incredibly strong. I refused to be a victim of my circumstances. I have the patience, I have the dedication and I have the guidance. 'I want to do all I can. I've come this far and I want to keep trying. It's still hard to believe I have so many complications just from a virus.'

'Shingles is vicious. It's like an inflammatory sizzling of the nerve. It seems too benign to cause so much yet it is so multifaceted. People get shingles, but in the head, that's different,' she said.

'To this day I don't understand how I'm still alive. I've always believed I can get through anything in life, but for the first five years no part of me believed I could sustain this long term.' I knew a certain amount of coping came from instinct but memories of how frightened I felt haunt me. 'Now, with the relief I have, whatever I'm capable of on any given day, I do it. It changes from one day to the next so I'm careful not to be forceful with myself because of lost time trying to survive,' I disclosed.

Days, months and years had passed me by, and I felt the pull to make up for lost time, finding it difficult to resist the instinct to push myself. 'Instead of focusing on how to overcome pain, I let the pain happen naturally and focus on how I can just *be* with it. It's a challenge to get the balance right.'

'It's part of the natural process that comes as you are able to demote the pain relative to other things you want to do with your life,' she explained. 'Enjoying family, enjoying productivity, you can only do that when you've demoted the pain. It doesn't come by denying the pain, or from a language of pretending everything is okay, but it does come from conscious decisions not to promote it.'

Late in 2023, I walked into her appointment room after returning from a holiday in the warmth to escape the winter. I could barely contain my tears of happiness when I shared I had managed a bike ride with my daughter and husband. The feeling of being back on a bike had been exhilarating. Despite the tears streaming down my face as I had watched my husband and daughter in front of me, I experienced pure joy in that moment. While I had hoped to achieve this goal, I had held no expectation. Each achievement, particularly with physical activity, was slowly helping me reclaim parts of my identity.

I had come a long way in my face pain journey, finally finding ways to live alongside it. I learnt that provided I patiently continued rehabilitation therapy from all angles, I could maintain improved function in my face to enhance my quality of life. Ongoing therapy slowly enabled my face to move with somewhat less pain so that I could laugh, talk, eat and smile more comfortably. While it still tired, drooped and dribbled, the improvements made my company more enjoyable and deepened the sense of connection I felt when spending time with friends and family. With a bank of coping strategies, the power of my mind and CBD, I believed pain and I could hold hands and walk this path together, *if* I listened to my body and *if* old beliefs were laid to rest.

31.

THE GAP

> *'A deep sense of love and belonging is an irreducible need of all people. We are biologically, cognitively, physically and spiritually wired to love, to be loved, and to belong. When those needs are not met, we don't function as we were meant to. We break. We fall apart. We numb. We ache. We hurt others. We get sick.'*
> Brené Brown

With more effective treatments in place and the small yet noticeable shift in my physical pain, I finally had the mental capacity and courage to focus on my emotional healing. It was time to step into the world of healing my past trauma. I had lost all confidence in myself despite the personal growth work I had done. My lifelong fears and beliefs remained stubbornly persistent, if not more intense, as I gained capacity for returning some normalcy to life. I wanted to put a stop to my automatic protective behaviours that were no longer serving me.

With little energy for actively contributing to the lives of others, my self-esteem and self-worth remained at an all-time low. Shame clung to me like a dark shadow. It was always lurking. I felt of no value. After seven bouts of shingles, my body had sent me a clear message that I could no longer sustain my people pleasing behaviours. I was exhausted. Tired of masking my pain and my truth, my limited energy needed to be put to better use.

Before I began EMDR trauma therapy, I undertook a three-month one-on-one trauma education program with an educational therapist. It was designed to deepen my understanding of trauma rather than provide therapy. The education program helped me acknowledge, accept and understand the impact of the trauma I had experienced. Revelations were difficult to digest, uncovering aspects of my life and self I either hadn't recognised or had denied, the pain of acknowledgement too unbearable.

Hameed Ali believes, 'What often happens is people come across their inner pain and see it as something to bypass rather than deal with their suffering, leaving undigested material in the psyche that left unfinished, usually comes back to bite you.' He also adds, 'The work with the wounding exposes a certain kind of gap, an emptiness.'[9]

The gap, the raw emptiness, was excruciating. But it marked the threshold of real change. Many months into therapy, I finally came face-to-face with the original wound behind my beliefs. Closing my eyes as the therapist guided me back, emotions bubbled to the surface under her gentle guidance. I felt myself physically try and pull away, as though wanting to deny the image of sick two-year-old me locked in a room. From the reality. From the feelings it evoked. But I couldn't. I wanted them to stop, to prevent my body from experiencing them. But there was no preventing the cascading release of excruciating emotions. They swept through me like a vicious tornado, tearing me apart as they moved through my body. The emotional charge released years of pain, almost too difficult to tolerate. Yet, the peace that came in the days and weeks that followed, was incomprehensible. My body finally allowed itself to release emotions that I had subconsciously suppressed my entire life.

I had finally reached the core. A deeply painful abandonment wound that had held me hostage my entire life. Unmet cries from the locked bedroom as a child had left a deep subconscious wound that had manifested throughout my life as the belief I was a burden, unworthy of love, comfort and nurture. A belief that I had to push through alone, be stoic and endure without complaint, despite the desperate desire to be comforted.

Now, through adult eyes, I could also see my mother's pain. Frozen by her own trauma every time I fell ill, fearing she would lose me. I could feel only inexplicable compassion for her pain. For her silence. It was impossible to suppress the surge of emotions over the following weeks. Finally, I gave myself permission to feel and release them fully as unrelenting tears streamed for my mother's pain and for the pain sustained by little two-year-old me.

For months, I wandered through my days lost. Empty. It felt like life would never be the same again. Initially I could not put words to the internal shift, but as time passed, I likened it to a baby taking its first steps. First unsteady, then experiencing a taste of freedom, yet, still uncertain. Still searching for safety, for what's known. Or perhaps a butterfly emerging, no longer confined. Free to explore a new world, a new way of being.

As my awareness and understanding of my protective behaviours increased through months of trauma therapy, it revealed why I had spent much of my life on high alert, always anticipating and mitigating potential threats to my emotional wellbeing. I learnt that my sensitivity to subtle changes in others' moods, expressions, behaviours and body language, guided me in how to keep safe – when to keep busy, when to withdraw and when to keep others happy. I learnt my protective strategies in childhood were in fact acts of bravery, essential for my survival then, and part of my growth now. This new perspective gave me a deeper understanding of my past and its impact on my present.

Instead of feeling ashamed of my sensitivities and protective behaviours, I learnt to offer myself self-compassion. For the first time, I could celebrate, love and embrace my sensitivity. It was the part of me that instinctively noticed and deeply felt the emotional experiences and states of others with empathy and compassion. It also helped me understand why I was so deeply affected by the suffering of others and the weight of atrocities. Embracing my sensitivity as a strength marked a significant shift in my healing. My protective behaviours were no longer required.

Throughout my journey, I had berated myself relentlessly to get on with life to avoid being a drag on others, despite the nagging desire to feel understood and nurtured. In doing this, I had denied *myself* validation for my dire circumstances. As a child, I had interpreted being physically and emotionally isolated during illness as proof no-one cared about me. That I was a burden. A nuisance. This wound had resurfaced with a vengeance throughout my isolating journey. I looked for proof everywhere, for confirmation of the belief I was a burden. I withdrew, masked my pain and pushed through the unbearable wherever I believed I had seen, heard or felt I was an inconvenience. An obligation.

Denying myself validation of how devastating my experience was, and the belief I had to push through, led to a loss of trust in myself and others. I discovered this was a common experience for many who have endured trauma. *'After trauma the world becomes sharply divided between those who know and those who don't. People who have not shared the traumatic experience cannot be trusted, because they can't understand it.'*[10]

In one of the trauma education sessions, the therapist shared a pivotal insight, revealing the roots of my subconscious, protective, people pleasing strategies. 'You have denied your emotions because you learnt it was natural to regulate everyone else's emotions and disconnect from your own. You also learnt that if you had an emotional reaction, you wouldn't get looked after.'

As a child, my instinctive survival response was subconscious and automatic. I realise I had disconnected from my own emotions to maintain connection then, just as I was doing now. Gabor Maté, well-known for his expertise on trauma and child development, talks about the deep need for attachment versus the need to be authentic, to be ourselves. *'When children are confronted with this dilemma, that I can have my own feelings and my own reactions, but if I do, I will not be accepted. There's no contest. The authenticity gets sacrificed every time. So the surrender of authenticity is actually a brilliant adaptation ...'* Discussing the psychological adjustments we make to maintain our attachment relationships, he also says, *'... we're not even aware of them, we think we are them; we think that's our personality. We identify with them and since our survival was associated with these adaptations, it's terrifying to give them up – even in adulthood, if we are at all even conscious of them.*[11]

My journey taught me that, deep down, I had learnt to believe love was earnt by meeting the needs of others. So, I became the helper, the pleaser. I wore that mask like the queen wore her crown. It became the organising principle of my life, woven into my very identity. But taking my mask off, choosing authenticity, speaking my needs, and showing my emotions felt like a risk; one that threatened rejection. Even amidst the desperation and pain, being vulnerable threatened aloneness. Disconnecting from my own emotions, appearing stoic, showing up as others would like, would surely help me maintain connection.

Understanding that disconnecting from my emotions and prioritising those of others wasn't a flaw but a survival strategy was a turning point. Accepting this opened the door to healing, allowing me to reclaim my authenticity, value my emotions and understand my worthiness.

Over time, the trauma therapist unearthed many embedded beliefs and adaptations held hostage by my trauma wounds. As each wounding experience was revisited, I learnt where my beliefs came from. Memories that once felt like gaping wounds began to heal over many months of intense sessions. Once the healing had begun in earnest and new beliefs were installed, the changes I needed to make and the boundaries required for my own self-care became clear. Boundaries that suddenly created the opportunity for me to live freely by my own values, without the need to please. Boundaries that saw me prioritise my health needs and prevent over-giving. They became the norm and I began to feel the freedom of not just envisioning the life I wanted to live but living and breathing it. In the healing phase, setting boundaries did not come easily for me, but I began to see them as an expression of self-worth, not selfishness.

As the heavy weight of trauma lightened, and I experienced the taste of emotional freedom, I wanted more. The liberation was well worth the pain of the process.

Amid the gruelling experience, the chance to release the weight of shame was a powerful motivator. It had held me captive. Through EMDR and kinesiology, I released feelings of failure and a deeply negative sense of self. I came to see the truth, concealed beneath the shame. I was deeply worthy. With self-compassion as my new lens, I saw the world differently. I saw my past differently. I saw myself differently.

As I progressed, the role of self-compassion became a crucial element in my healing. Learning to treat myself with the same empathy and care I offered others was transformative. It softened the harsh self-judgements and allowed me to be patient with my progress. Self-compassion became a new source of strength, one that was nurturing rather than punishing.

Throughout my shingles journey, the desire to speak my needs and the fear of rejection were in constant conflict. My healing shed light on the root of this conflict, but it was reading the powerful words of Gabor Mate' that really struck a chord; '... a child whose cries are not responded to ... not held close to a parent's warm body when in distress, learns a clear if wordless lesson: that his needs will not be met, ... that he is not lovable as he is.'[12] I had lived my life believing this.

Releasing this belief allowed me to see with new insight and clarity what I was unable to perceive as an infant. My parents had indeed loved me. More than I could ever have known. However, with the early abandonment wound unhealed, I experienced the same pain each time I was ill and alone. Now, armed with new insight, I could learn to speak my needs and seek support with less fear.

The compassion and empathy I learnt to extend to myself were instrumental in my healing process. It was as much about compassionately nurturing my emotional world as it was about managing my physical pain. The fear of abandonment, once a persistent shadow, began to diminish as I provided myself with the emotional support and validation I had long sought from others.

Throughout my healing process, delving into the most painful experiences of my life to feel and release emotions stored in my body, I was more tender than ever. For months, I felt like a wounded soldier. Wounds poked during that period were so raw they barely needed a whisper to trigger an emotional response, each time directing me to where further healing was required. This period marked a profound turning point. It was not just about revisiting the past but transforming my relationship with it. A transition from surviving to truly living.

32.

A LIFE WORTH LIVING

*'While the world is falling apart,
she is unfolding into something beyond loss.'*
V. J. Markham

Sitting at my desk during the winter of 2024, a childhood photograph of myself stared back at me. The two-year-old girl in the picture looked so carefree, her smile a testament to the innocence of youth. For many years, looking at this image haunted me. Her face reminded me of the many sad times in her childhood. In that moment, however, I finally saw the face of a little girl who was incredibly brave. I felt only deep love and compassion for her.

My journey through pain and loss caused by the shingles virus ultimately led me to uncover and heal a deeply painful childhood wound that had impacted my life in ways beyond my understanding. With the strength and empowerment that the emotional healing gifted me, I can now approach my physical healing with self-compassion knowing I am doing the best I can.

While I continue to live with the pain from shingles, I have made carefully planned adjustments for the long term, allowing me to create a life worth living – albeit different from the one I had envisioned for myself. Each year, as the seasons shift and the cold sets in, a familiar dread of isolation and confinement creeps back in. To manage both the pain and the weight of winter, I continue to travel to warmer climates, finding solace in nature, exploring new sights and seeking refuge behind the lens of my camera. Self-love and self-care, once perceived as selfish, are now integral to daily life and directly reflect my quality of day-to-day living. Pain management strategies, pacing myself, yoga, mindfulness, breath work, an anti-inflammatory diet and CBD, are critical to my ongoing efforts to maintain a good life. Regular B12 injections and intravenous vitamin therapy continue to help boost my energy levels. Every day is an opportunity to advocate for myself and each activity I undertake becomes part of the delicate balance I work to maintain. Even photography, such a welcome distraction in the moment, can lead to pain and exhaustion afterward, triggered from squinting and intense concentration. The physical cost is a constant reminder that every choice must be carefully measured.

Finally, with pain less intense, my short-term memory has improved significantly – though frustratingly, I still often spend time looking for lost items. Some of the activities I once loved but thought would remain out of reach, I am enjoying once more. I can now play cards and board games with John, the girls and friends with enjoyment. Providing I manage my pain and fatigue, I drive once more with confidence.

Despite the many strategies I have in place, my focus still shifts back to the pain when I begin to tire or encounter specific environmental triggers. While I do my best, sometimes staying focused and present can still be a challenge. During these times, I often grow quiet, my gaze distant as I work to resist the sensations. Pressing a finger into my ear helps me cope with the intensity and rubbing my face distracts me somewhat from the crawling sensations or sharp pressure that lingers. I try to keep my mind stronger than the pain but sometimes I falter.

Managing the balance between pain management and freedom from the constraints of physical suffering and limitation is not a daily task, but an hourly one. With thoughtful pacing and careful planning, I enjoy increased social interactions, laughing, smiling and talking. I no longer stifle laughter, despite the pain it creates. It would seem like an odd thing to do, to inflict more torture on a face already suffering, but my ability to smile and laugh is a joyous way to express myself. It's important to my identity and always has been. It feeds my soul. To enjoy these seemingly simple joys, regular rehabilitation therapy with the wonderful team of therapists who support me remains imperative, giving me the best chance of improved function and increased stamina. They have done wonders for my social confidence. They are also important in undoing any setbacks or flare-ups caused if I overdo it. Just like a gym workout, but for my face, I continue the face and jaw exercises twice a day at home, along with exercises to assist my balance and dizziness. They are an essential part of my daily routine, as habitual as brushing my teeth.

In the same way emotional healing is not linear, neither is managing my physical pain. Both will continue to fluctuate like the weather. That's the reality of chronic pain – but I no longer try and run from it. It's a constant companion and I tend to it with love and care. I have no choice because PHTN and Ramsay Hunt recovery rates are poor, so I must accept their presence. I *do* look well, however behind my smile and laughter is extraordinary pain. Often my therapists have said, 'And yet you still smile.' I have moments of sadness and days I could scream from the rooftop at my pain, at what I've lost, *and* what I've gained but never asked for. While I try not to dwell there, I do occasionally give myself permission to be human and allow myself to mindfully feel and express the emotions that arise. I never have pain-free days and I still struggle with the balance of managing fatigue and keeping occupied enough to distract myself from it. It's a daily juggling act but I generally know my limits. Over time, I have learnt to accept and embrace pain management strategies as part of each day. I also have periods I need a break from appointments, and that's important too.

In the context of my unwavering commitment to making the best of my situation, I am grateful for the gift of my determined spirit, the life experiences that tested me, and an upbringing that instilled in me the power of perseverance. I begin each day with a fierce determination to create a life worth living and will continue my internal drive toward constant improvement. I love the reward this brings, even just being able to laugh, smile and eat chicken. And that cable knit blanket? I made it. It took almost two years and was unpicked too many times to count, but I made it.

In 2024, during our annual holiday at Smoky Bay we finally made the heartbreaking decision to relinquish ownership of Little Bet. In 2019, I recognised the need to simplify life moving forward, but I could not make that devastating decision then. I had denied I was no longer in a position to manage the mental or financial burden of maintaining it. The weight of that truth was crushing, but even heavier was the guilt. I felt solely responsible for what seemed like one of the most significant and painful losses to our family.

Just the thought of letting go of the shack was unbearable. It felt like severing a part of myself, an emotional and physical separation from memories of my mother. The idea of saying goodbye was excruciating but I also knew I would *never* feel ready. How could I?

My initial unwillingness to part with Little Bet clashed with my need to prioritise my wellbeing. It couldn't be a decision made from the heart, it had to come from the head. The strength I had gained through healing allowed me to face the emotions of this gut-wrenching decision. Painful experience had also taught me the consequences of neglecting my health and the importance of self-care.

In making the decision, I knew I was letting go of something I was emotionally unprepared for, but I also felt a new strength beyond my sadness. No longer hiding from the truth, I found the courage to face what had been too difficult to contemplate. I needed to reduce responsibilities. I had no choice.

Leaving there in April, my tears were unstoppable. Shack memories persistently resurfaced throughout the long drive back to Adelaide. Sobbing, I turned to John repeatedly and asked, 'Are you sure we're doing the right thing?' The decision felt unbearable.

But no matter how painful, no exchange of property or loss of possessions could ever take away my mother's presence in my heart. Memories of her would live on regardless, and in time I would find other ways to keep them alive.

I hold on to hope my stamina will continue to slowly increase, along with improved sleep and less pain and fatigue. I have learnt the hard way the reality of neuro and viral fatigue. My brain gets tired trying to figure out how to do things that it once did with automaticity. My body is constantly trying to heal from this virus, and that alone makes me tired. Unfortunately, it is not a week-long virus.

I feel gratitude for my life each day, and in some ways, even for shingles. Though it took so much, it also gifted me a life-changing, life-giving healing journey for which I can only be grateful. It taught me that while many problems *can* be solved, some simply require acceptance and in fact they may even be the solution to a problem you were unaware of. It taught me the importance of self-love, self-care and self-compassion. While life has shrunk compared to how I lived pre-shingles, ironically, the internal shifts have made it seem much bigger. More peaceful.

I have learnt to live by realistic expectations based on my capabilities. I try not to overextend myself and have released the shame around not giving in the same way I once could. One day, I shared with a friend my pain at not being able to give much over the past few years. Laughing in disbelief, she said, 'You did give. Through your pain and suffering you gave us so much more than you know. Sharing your journey helped us; your determination and perseverance taught us so much and gave us strength in our own lives. Your ability to forgive taught us forgiveness of others and of ourselves.'

I had overlooked an important aspect of my journey. Giving comes in many forms. I could give simply by being myself. Instead of focusing on a 'to do' list, it was time to focus on a 'to be' list.

Reflecting on the image of my two-year-old self, I realised my pursuit to find purpose was in the healing process itself. What better purpose is there beyond healing and finding your authentic self? As I look each day at that image, I remind that little girl: 'Enough suffering. You can rest now. You don't have to try so hard anymore to put on a brave face, to pretend you're okay when you're not. You *can* express your needs. You are the only one who truly knows your suffering, and you are the only one you need to listen to. Doing does not equal love. You are loved simply for being you. You are enough. You are exactly where you need to be.'

AFTERWORD

'And once the storm is over, you won't remember how you made it through, how you managed to survive. You won't even be sure whether the storm is really over. But one thing is certain. When you come out of the storm, you won't be the same person who walked in. That's what this storm's all about.'
Haruki Murakami

We can sometimes wrestle with the idea that life is happening *for* us, not *to* us. Letting go of what was and embracing what is can feel impossible, especially when answers remain out of reach. But life doesn't always make sense in the moment nor pause while we feel ourselves unravelling. It demands us to keep moving and does not promise a perfect resolution.

And yet, within this absence of a resolution lies an opening, an opportunity for growth to unfold, strength to emerge and the quiet grace of our own resilience to surface. Here, we discover our capacity to heal. Rather than being defined by what we have lost, we learn to find peace, shape our own closure and step forward with new understanding.

We are not merely survivors of our storms; we are the authors of our own healing, even in the midst of uncertainty. And the meaning we seek? That is ours to define.

'Somewhere between what she survived, and who she was becoming, was exactly where she was meant to be. She was starting to love the journey and find the comfort in the quiet corners of her wildest dreams. They say people don't change ... Well, she wasn't always this way. Even if she did not change the entire world, she would change her part of it. And she would affect the people she shared it with. A butterfly whose wings have been touched, can indeed still fly. Whether something was meant to be, or meant to leave, didn't matter as much anymore. She would soak up the sun, kiss the breeze, and she would fly regardless.'

J Raymond
(Published with permission from the author)

ACKNOWLEDGEMENTS

'In hard times, people don't want to be told to look on the bright side. They want to know you're on their side. Even if you can't help them feel better, you can always help them feel seen. The best way to support others is not to cheer them up. It's to show up.'
Adam Grant

Acknowledging those who have shown up throughout my journey, helping me reach a place where I can live with PHTN pain in a way that feels worthwhile, is both humbling and deeply emotional. For the first five and a half years, I truly believed this cruel pain would claim my life. But at pivotal moments, people stepped in, some knowingly, others without realising the difference they were making, helping prevent what once felt inevitable.

I did not arrive here on my own. It has taken unwavering support from a team of medical professionals, various therapists, friends and family to help me find ways to coexist with pain, and a growing willingness to stay open and vulnerable.

Though I cannot name every person, I hope these words honour the ways, both great and small, you contributed to my healing and gave me a reason to keep going.

To my husband and daughters – words will never be enough. No mother wants to be the fallen one, unable to be the pillar of strength her family relies on, or worse, the cause of their suffering. Thank you for loving me when I couldn't love myself and for holding on to hope when mine had faded. You are, and always will be, the reason I continue to find the strength to continue. For that, I am eternally grateful. You are so deeply loved.

To my friends and family – thank you for staying beside me in the face of helplessness and uncertainty. I am forever grateful for your patience as I grappled with immense grief and loss and the relentless reality of pain. Thank you for your unwavering presence, even when you didn't know what to say or do. Your calls, visits, walks, organising social activities and moments of simply being there brought light into my life, especially during John's time away. Your compassion, kindness and acceptance of my limitations gave me space to be as I am, not as I used to be. Regular human connection has truly been the thread that kept and continues to keep me going.

To my wonderful GP – my angel – thank you for your patience and unwavering belief in me. You held space through the darkest moments and delivered truths I didn't want to hear but needed to. Thank you for listening, for guiding me to the right people, for never giving up, for honouring my choice to remain medication-free and for always keeping it real.

To Professor Goss – your communication with my wider medical team, your honesty, validation and encouraging words made a lasting difference. I am especially grateful for your time in reading this book, helping with the glossary and ensuring medical accuracy.

To every therapist, doctor and specialist who stood alongside me – thank you for trying everything in your power to ease my suffering. Your knowledge, compassion and persistence were deeply felt, even when treatment brought pain or hard truths.

To my neurophysiotherapist – thank you for restoring my social confidence. Your work helped me regain the ability to laugh, smile and eat with greater ease. Unexpectedly, I came to look forward to our sessions despite the pain. They not only became a path to regaining my confidence, but also a space of healing and understanding.

To my craniosacral and myofascial therapist – thank you for your ongoing support and the much-needed relief you bring to

ACKNOWLEDGEMENTS

my fiery nerves, particularly after table tennis. Wednesdays are my favourite day of the week.

To Astrid and Lilian – your work took me down a life-changing path of healing I never imagined. The internal shifts I have made and the peace I now carry are a testament to your care. Thank you for holding me so gently through a process that was both painful and freeing.

To Heidi – you appeared, again and again, just when I needed you most. I now understand what it means when people speak of *the gift of Heidi*. I have been lucky enough to receive that gift many times. You didn't just change my life, you saved it. I'll be forever grateful.

To my betta readers and editors, Marinda, Michaela, Jenny K, Jenny B, Kris, Lisa, Raelene and Sarah – thank you for taking on the difficult and generous task of offering feedback to help shape this book. Your insights and suggestions were invaluable, and I'm deeply grateful for the time and care you gave to help make it what it is.

Jenny K, your support through the entire editing journey, whether sitting beside me, over the phone or pouring over my manuscript alone, meant everything. Your thoughtful and methodical reading, your honesty, care and persistence helped me bring this story to life. You pushed me to write what I wanted to avoid. Thank you for not letting me get away with it and for helping me create a book I'm now proud of.

Lisa, thank you not only for your incredible love and support, but for bravely challenging me to rework the initial and final chapters of this book. With your steady loving presence, you helped me find the words I thought I couldn't speak, let alone write. Thank you for helping me bring them to life and for staying by my side through the tears and doubt.

To Natalie – for quietly and gently guiding me in the right direction when I was incapable of making clear-headed decisions for myself. Your support and persistence were pivotal to helping me find ways to improve my quality of life.

To the Ultimate 48-Hour Author publishing team – thank you for your ongoing support. You gave me the courage to persist when I lost belief in myself and this book.

Each of you, in your own way, helped me find the strength to keep going. For that, I'm eternally grateful.

'Connection is the energy that exists between people when they feel seen, heard and valued; when they can give and receive without judgement; and when they derive sustenance and strength from the relationship.'
Brené Brown

ABOUT THE AUTHOR

Denise Trewartha grew up with her parents and two siblings in Nunjikompita, a remote farming community on the Far West Coast of South Australia, on the traditional lands of the Wirangu people. Her childhood playground was the vast, open landscape, fostering a deep love for the outdoors. She attended a small, one-teacher primary school with 14–16 students before attending boarding school in Adelaide.

Raised in a close-knit farming community, Denise developed a strong commitment to service and contribution, values she has carried throughout her life. She was awarded a School Service Award in her final year of college (1985), Ceduna's Australia Day Junior Citizen of the Year (1989) and received a NEITA (National Excellent in Teaching Award) for service to her school community (2004).

Denise has a teaching degree and worked in various teaching roles and as a literacy consultant. Passionate about the role of interconnectedness, she instilled the belief that 'we are in this together' in her classroom – a philosophy she continues to uphold in her life, believing it builds resilience, enhances wellbeing and fosters compassion for shared human experiences. This concept of common humanity also inspired her memoir, *But You Look So Well*, written to give voice to those who suffer in silence so they feel seen, heard and understood. Later, driven by a deep curiosity about human behaviour, she pursued postgraduate education in life coaching, further exploring how connection shapes personal growth and resilience.

She is married with two wonderful daughters and now resides in Adelaide, South Australia. Despite living with a chronic pain condition, Denise remains deeply connected to nature, spending as much time outdoors as her health allows, travelling to warmer climates in winter. Denise continues to serve her community, visiting health facilities with her adored cavoodle, Gracie, to provide pet therapy. Through her memoir and community work, she hopes to inspire others to embrace the power of interconnectedness in creating compassionate, supportive communities.

TESTIMONIAL

Facial pain has been my companion for more than 15 years. It has kept me company during my teen years, young adult years and now into my thirties.

When TN entered my life at 17 years old, I had no idea the impact it would have on me. It would take nearly a decade to have my diagnosis and with it some pain relief. The strength to live without relief from the pain of TN is a strength like no other.

TN pain is horrific. Some days, I am unable to talk, eat or even move without the stabbing electrical shocks that strike my face over and over again.

When TN entered my life, I truly thought my life was over. I did not dare to dream of a beautiful future, let alone one without pain. What I didn't know then that I do know now, is that even with TN, life can be beautiful. TN did not steal from me a beautiful future.

I am continuously learning to embrace the joy amongst the pain.

Laura
Fellow TN warrior from Hampton Roads, Virginia

GLOSSARY

Trigeminal Neuralgia – A chronic nerve pain condition that causes what is often described as severe shooting, stabbing, burning and/ or aching pain in the distribution of the trigeminal nerve.

Types:

Idiopathic Trigeminal Neuralgia – The most common type. Once thought to be of unknown origin and hence, 'idiopathic', now commonly thought to be from vascular compression of the trigeminal ganglion.

Secondary Trigeminal Neuralgia – Secondary to injury to the nerve from trauma or pathology.

Post Herpetic Trigeminal Neuralgia (PHTN) – Develops following a shingles outbreak, where the herpes zoster virus establishes itself in the trigeminal nerve.

Trigeminal Neuropathy – As well as the pain of trigeminal neuralgia, there is also numbness or change in sensation. This is associated with either injury or pathology such as a brain tumour.

Ramsay Hunt syndrome – A condition affecting the facial nerve following a shingles outbreak. It typically begins with herpes zoster vesicles in the external ear, followed by facial weakness or facial palsy. In some cases, other cranial nerves may also be involved. Ear pain, tinnitus and hearing loss may also be present.

The diagnosis of these various neurological conditions requires a thorough specialist evaluation, including history-taking, examination and imaging. This can be followed by targeted treatments.

BIBLIOGRAPHY

Albrecht, M.A. (2024, February 16). *Patient education: Shingles (Beyond the Basics)*. Retrieved from UpToDate: https://www.uptodate.com/contents/shingles-beyond-the-basics

Cleveland Clinic. (2024). *Facial Nerve*. Retrieved from Cleveland Clinic: https://my.clevelandclinic.org/health/body/22218-facial-nerve

Commune. (n.d.). *A Return to Wholeness with Dr Gabor Maté*. Retrieved March 2024, from One Commune: https://www.onecommune.com/a-return-to-wholeness-dr-gabor-mate-workshop

Davis, S., Cooke, N., & Sutton, J. (2015). *Rewire Your Pain*. Perth: WA Specialist Pain Services.

Howard, A. (2024). *Trauma and Awakening*. Retrieved May 2024, from Conscious Life: https://trauma.consciouslife.com/videos/

Kolk, B. A. (2015). *The Body Keeps the Score: Brain, Mind, and Body in the Healing of Trauma*. New York: Penguin Books Limited.

Maté, G., & Maté, D. (2022). *The Myth of Normal - Illness, Health and Healing in a Toxic Culture*. London, United Kingdom: Vermilion.

Naveen, K. N., Pradeep, A. V., Kumar, J. S., Hegde, S. P., Pai, V. V., & Athanikar, S. B. (2014, July). *Herpes zoster affecting all three divisions of trigeminal nerve in an immunocompetent male: a rare presentation*. Retrieved from National Library of Medicine: https://pmc.ncbi.nlm.nih.gov/articles/PMC4103307/

Niemeyer, C.S., Harlander-Locke, M., Bubak, A.N., Rzasa-Lynn, R., Birlea, M. (2024, January 23). *Trigeminal Postherpetic Neuralgia: From Pathophysiology to Treatment.* Retrieved from National Library of Medicine: https://pmc.ncbi.nlm.nih.gov/articles/PMC10940365/#CR9

Pilitsis, J. G., & Khazan, O. (2024, April). *Trigeminal Neuralgia.* Retrieved from American Association of Neurological Surgeons: https://www.aans.org/patients/conditions-treatments/trigeminal-neuralgia/

Raymond, J. (2016). *Spades.* CreateSpace Independent Publishing Platform.

Sampathkumar, P. D., Drage, L. A., & Martin, D. P. (2009, March). *Herpes zoster (shingles) and postherpetic neuralgia.* Retrieved from National Library of Medicine: https://pmc.ncbi.nlm.nih.gov/articles/PMC2664599/#S6

ENDNOTES

1. (Cleveland Clinic, 2024)
2. (Mary A Albrecht, 2024)
3. (Niemeyer CS, 2024)
4. (Cleveland Clinic, 2024)
5. (Naveen, et al., 2014)
6. (Sampathkumar, Drage, & Martin, 2009)
7. (Pilitsis & Khazan, 2024)
8. (Davis, Cooke, & Sutton, 2015, p. 89)
9. (Howard, 2024)
10. (Kolk, 2015, p. 18)
11. (Commune, n.d.)
12. (Maté & Maté, 2022, p. 131)

www.ingramcontent.com/pod-product-compliance
Lightning Source LLC
Chambersburg PA
CBHW020403080526
44584CB00014B/1151